Nat is a comedian, rock musician, mental health advocate
and award-winning, bestselling author.

Nat's platform has enabled him to hold up a tongue-in-cheek mirror
to antiquated cultural norms, to promote kindness and to share
his battle with anxiety and depression, collecting him a dedicated
audience of over 3.5 million thanks to his message of positivity and
inclusivity that has resonated with champions the world over.

When he's not filming, cooking or foraging for rosemary,
Nat can often be found indulging his love of rock'n'roll and comedy,
playing in various bands and stand-up rooms around Australia.
He is the author of two bestselling books, *Un-cook Yourself*
and *Death to Jar Sauce*, which were both shortlisted at the
Australian Book Industry Awards and won the Booktopia Favourite
Australian Book Award in 2020 and 2021 respectively, with Nat
donating the proceeds each time to Beyond Blue.

🅕 @natswhatireckon
📷 @nats_what_i_reckon
▶️ @natswhatireckon
♪ @natswhatireckon

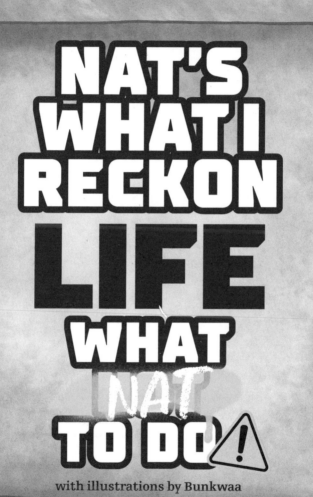

NAT'S WHAT I RECKON LIFE WHAT NAT TO DO ⚠

with illustrations by Bunkwaa

EBURY PRESS

UK | USA | Canada | Ireland | Australia
India | New Zealand | South Africa | China

Ebury Press is part of the Penguin Random House group of companies whose addresses can be found at global.penguinrandomhouse.com.

Penguin
Random House
Australia

First published by Ebury Press, 2022

Text copyright © Nat's What I Reckon, 2022
Internal illustrations © Bunkwaa, 2022

The moral right of the author has been asserted.

Cover photography and internal photos of Nat by Julia Gee
Cover images: graffiti spray paint by shutterstock.com/Igor Vitkovskiy;
    marble bust by shutterstock.com/Gilmanshin
Cover, text design and typesetting by Adam Laszczuk © Penguin Random House Australia

Printed and bound in Australia by Griffin Press, an accredited
ISO ANZ/NZS 14001 Environmental Management Systems printer

A catalogue record for this
book is available from the
NATIONAL LIBRARY
OF AUSTRALIA National Library of Australia

ISBN 978 1 76104 983 5

penguin.com.au

MIX
Paper from
responsible sources
FSC® C009448

We at Penguin Random House Australia acknowledge that Aboriginal and Torres Strait Islander peoples are the first storytellers and Traditional Custodians of the land on which we live and work. We honour Aboriginal and Torres Strait Islander peoples' continuous connection to Country, waters, skies and communities. We celebrate Aboriginal and Torres Strait Islander stories, traditions and living cultures; and we pay our respects to Elders past and present.

Listen up, champions. The information contained in the book is of a general nature and you should seek advice from a medical professional instead of my opinionated waffle.

I dedicate this book to anyone struggling with their mental health.

CONTENTS

Introduction: What's Garnon, Champion? 1

1. Live Laugh Love Man Cave 5

2. Good Vibes Only 19

3. What's the Worst That Could Happen? 33

4. Keep Your Friends Close and Your Enemies Closer 45

5. Man Up 57

6. No Pain, No Gain 71

7. Sleep More 83

8. An Apple a Day Keeps the Doctor Away 99

9. What Doesn't Kill You Makes You Stronger 113

10. Focus More 125

11. Stay in School 137

12. Everything Happens for a Reason 149

13. Dance Like No One is Watching 161

14. Someone Has It Worse Than You 173

15. Life is Short and YOLO so Live Every Day Like it's Your Last and Carpe Diem, Please! 187

Final Shit Sayings Showdown 199

Conclusion: Check Ya Later, Skater 203

Contributors 205

Resources & Acknowledgements 206

WHAT'S GARNON, CHAMPION?

This is the bit where I introduce the book to you and you get to decide whether it's a shit idea to read it or not. Maybe you read the other two I wrote and thought I could have done a little better, so you're back for the third effort hoping that I don't cook it this time?

Whatever the reason, here goes the big sell . . .

Let me ask you this: does it give you the major fucken shits when some random wannabe hero notices you're not smiling the way they'd like and dishes you some verbal trash such as 'You know it takes more effort to frown than it does to smile!'? Does it ever give you the Jiminy Crickets having to read all the fucking annoying positive affirmations plastered over the walls of your local café? Does it make you wanna puke and explode into flames all at once when some arsehole tells you to make lemonade out of lemons?

If the answer to any of these is yes, then champion, you have come to the right place. I have spent a lifetime downloading unsolicited, cringey and superfluous life tips from all sorts of scenarios, everywhere from placemats to people. How are we as champions with complex personalities and unique lives supposed to deal with being constantly bulldozed by such stupid sayings that have little to no modern relevance to the situation at hand?

How do people fucken keep getting away with it?!
I've had a gutful of shit advice.

'Everything is meant to be.' Oh really? Meant to be what?
'Smile more, you'll be happier!'

How about ya mind your own lack of compassionate business?

And why is Carpe Diem a shockingly great call?

It's not!

It's nonsense like this that's just a flowery way to say something you already knew was an option but might not be in a position to act on right now. Thanks for the Carpe Diem idea, champ, but did you ever stop to consider that I could be a little overwhelmed right now and what's seizing my day is more like a series of panic attacks, so I'm not hugely available for double black diamond runs, skydiving and climbing Mount Everest? Calm down, mate.

This is why I wanted to write this book. I've collected some of the worst examples of exhausting old annoying prattle and broken them down with large doses of my bloody opinion and the occasional mental health chat. Some could argue that I am in fact guilty of doing the very same thing I'm critiquing by dishing out all these unrequested hot takes, but I assume that by picking up this book you're down for hearing me sound off about them. To put it simply, it's a bit of a 'take it or leave it' kinda vibe, so Carpe Book, eh?

I do have a fucking lot of opinions, and I do like to swear a lot so there is a bit of that going on, particularly about issues I consider to be bullshit or need to be had a chat about. I have made a career out of demonstrating how unnecessary and over the top a lot of the 'normal' things are in life, so that's what gave me the big idea of writing a book about them. A lot of my carrying-on has been in the kitchen, which brings me to my next point and one that may shock you:

This isn't a cookbook. Soz about it!

This information may be a touch jarring (lol) for a few readers out there who find themselves asking 'Hang on, aren't you that fucken long-haired YouTube bloke who does all the swearing and cooking things?' While that is true and while that part is totally rad, not everything I do revolves around cooking. BUT ALAS that's not to say I don't have something to offer in that department. I have written one of those cookbook things. It's called *Death to Jar Sauce* and it's sick if I don't mind saying so myself, which it seems I don't. So champion, if it's cookbooks you're looking for then never fear, I have your back: it's bright pink, filled with sick illustrations and has flames on the cover so you won't miss it. In fact, I have *another* fucken book that's yellow and has recipes in it as well, so if you prefer the colour yellow then this is sterling news.

I have to do a simultaneous horn-tootin' and thank-you combo for helping those two books win Favourite Australian Book of the Year Award two years in a row! Fucken hell, what ripper news, thanks gang.

So hopefully these few paragraphs have sold you on the idea that this book won't be total shit. Obviously I'm going to tell you it's fucken awesome, but that is for you to make your own mind up about. Please enjoy (or put back on the shelf).

PARTY ON
ROCK ON OR F**KOFF!
YEAH
CUT SICK
LIVE
LAUGH
LOVE
MAN
CAVE

Let's just say that as I walk into Ian and Dianne's house, very early on I am made aware by Ian of the 'better part' of the house where all the cool shit is. It is filled with numerous intense objects: on the personal tour, I'm maybe shown a Jack Daniel's fridge, an actual bar, a Jim Beam flag, several faux rusted old gas station items, a jukebox, a front fender and several vintage number plates from cars Ian never owned, a bikini calendar and several shit sexist signs.

Oh god, the signs. One of them has a warning on it letting me know to beware that I have entered the very scary MAN CAVE.

Beneath it, there's a list of ten equally concerning rules for the cave:

MAN CAVE RULES
My Cave, My Rules
All Chick Flicks Banned
No Bitching, No Issues
Talking About Feelings Gets A Lifetime Ban
Man Controls All Remotes
Man is Always Right
Eat Bacon
Women by Invitation Only
Sports Channel 24/7
Flatulence Allowed

Wow, what the pretend caveman fuck is all that?

Bit intense, don't ya think? These man cave rules are entirely stressful and weird. It's like I've time-travelled back to 1987, when life was worse. The whole place is giving off the strongest vibes that it wants to be back there, so it kind of makes sense. Who needs progressive society anyway, right?

I have thousands of political and identity issues with the list of rules, the worst of which are the heavily woman-hating ones that say 'women have to do what men want'. Just fucken disgusting. The concept of a cave in a garage I find for many reasons claustrophobic, so I tend to avoid man caves at all costs. However, I did go to a man cave expo and made a video about it with Jules once, which was pretty funny.

JULES' TAKE ON THE MAN CAVE EXPO

The Man Cave Expo was a weird experience. The amount of turbo-masc products available for purchase was pretty funny – such as intense boxing set-ups that probably won't get used, everything in black with sports stripes so it goes faster (I guess), and accessories and memorabilia for hobbies men are told they're all supposed to *like* (fishing, sportsball, drinking like a fish while watching sportsball), and of course heavy machinery. Because you are definitely going to be putting a forklift in your garage.

It was a mixed bag for me. Some of it seemed a little bit sad because it was so deeply clichéd, like the bravado-laden 'No Chicks Allowed' signs and Big Mouth Billy Bass electronic singing fish, but then there was also a LOL and a sweetness there when you started getting into the thick of it. Think ninja swords to fulfil your childhood badass fantasies, and some sci-fi/wizard-themed accessories that you can finally feel okay to admit you like because you're an adult and this is YOUR ROOM FOR YOUR STUFF. Which is maybe what you really want, rather than a dick-swinging hovel?

And, you know, I think it's important to have interests that differ from your partner's – you should nurture whatever your hobbies are, and having space to do that is really valuable. But how much more empowering is it when it's free from gendered bullshit? Lean into what you really love, free yourself from the shackles of what the patriarchy tells you is good for a 'man' or a 'woman'. Have the weightlifting rig next to your Barbie collection. Put your signed UFC posters above the Animal Crossing memorabilia shrine. And pleeease take down any pro-bro signs. It might be 'your' room, but you should want to welcome the women and gender nonconforming people in your life into the world you're creating. Remember that you already occupy heaps of space. Cis, straight men, I'm looking at you.

I have also been annoyed at many cafés, hotel rooms and bars where they proudly display signs chock-full of well-meaning yet utterly empty affirmations. Live, Laugh, Love . . . yikes.

Nice and all, but being told to 'Live, Laugh, Love' by a piece of wood is not the breakthrough tip I need today. Besides, it's been flogged to death since the late noughties, and is as corny as a YouTuber starting a video with 'What's going on, guys?' That's not even a question, is it? It's an empty conversation gap-filler bunch of words used to indicate that you are using as little of your brain as possible and have very little care for the person you're talking to. I feel that 'Live, Laugh, Love' is in the same basket; it's as overused as a Coldplay soundtrack on insurance ads.

All of these shitty wooden-sign sayings are supposed

to remind you to do shit that you already knew was a good idea, but to me they come across more like a demand than a gentle nudge to 'love' something out of nowhere. Don't you think it's a little entitled to start dishing out your positivity diarrhoea everywhere? Let's say that someone might have had a fucken rotter of a day, right? Maybe they crashed their car, couldn't afford the insurance to fix their car or the other person's, they both really need their cars to get to work otherwise they will lose their jobs and then they won't be able to pay rent and won't have anywhere to live – but your shit-hot master advice in that moment is to just love that shit a little more, ya dickhead. There is nothing worth laughing about when you crash your car, particularly if someone is injured. And nor does the situation call for more existence – you do not need to do any more living right in this moment.

Surely someone has to be held accountable for the fucken annoying wooden sign waving its finger telling me to do shit from the mantelpiece/above the bar/on the toilet door! No matter what goes on in that space, it's the same set of words for every moment of the day just hanging there telling you the same thing, so smugly certain it's never a bad idea to do what it says.

When the family is having a big barney at the Christmas table, a moment you knew was going to happen since last Boxing Day, where is the sign that will bring peace and contentment? RIGHT THERE! Why doesn't someone just point to it and yell out what it says? 'Can't we just live, laugh, love, everyone?' That's its job, isn't it? Should we not all obey the sign if it sits so high up above us all? If it's your sign then surely you should be willing to follow its didactic demands even if in some of these moments it's totally inappropriate? I feel bullied by it, it's poorly timed, and I reckon in a way it contributed to the uncomfortable vibe in here.

These dreadful signs are a dime a dozen. How many trees needed to get cut down to help remind us the 'Beach' is nearby? I understand that it's supposed to bring a bit of joy into the room, but it doesn't for me. I walk in and immediately have something to read that tells me how I'm feeling is incorrect.

'Live, Laugh, Love' is only one of a bunch of these hang 'em and tell 'em signs that I've seen in my travels. Here are some other punishers:

'BE HAPPY'

Excuse me, could you just calm the fuck down with this turbo shit: telling me to be happy is fucken rude, let alone when commanded to do so by a sign from the two-dollar shop. I will experience the emotion that is appointed to me by my unsteady brain, thank you very much.

'CHILL'

You chill!

'BREATHE'

Possibly the most useful and useless advice all at once by virtue of the fact you're already doing it just by existing. Gee whiz, you come up with that idea yourself? As someone who is no stranger to panic attacks, this advice is quite useful in the middle of one, but it's also a reminder that I will probably have one later anyway.

'THINK, DO, BE POSITIVE'

Not only am I thinking, but I am doing myself a stress headache reading this nonsense telling me to be what I am already trying to be.

'THIS IS OUR HAPPY PLACE'

I love this for you, but I don't heaps need to know all this personal info. I have a lot going on and downloading your bio to my brain isn't high on my to-do list.

'YOU ARE UNLIMITED'

I know that movie came out a while back where everyone had some kind of strange pinger and became 'unlimited' or whatever, but that movie wasn't a documentary and nor was *The Matrix*, sorry.

'DREAM'

Unless you smoke heaps of marijuana, this shouldn't be an issue. It certainly doesn't warrant looming down from a wall at a café.

'KEEP CALM AND DRINK COFFEE'

Okay righto, we get it, you drink coffee a lot. Might have something to do with why you slept like shit last night and are now in such a bad mood that the sign is the only thing that knows how you feel.

And the list goes on . . .

There is a point at which I think it is healthy to accept that just because you're in a good mood, it doesn't mean everyone else is or should be right now. It's nice that you are happy, we all want that too. Anyone who's ever been around someone bombed on booze or MDMA will be all too familiar with the way live-laugh-love energy can do your head in. And what's worse is if you push back at ALL against the living and the loving and the laughing, you're made to feel like a demon load of shit, as though you're what's wrong with Earth. 'Awww come on, it's not that bad is it?'

Yeah mate, it *is* that bad, and you're making it worse.

I understand the intended purpose of all these wannabe motivational signs is to either make people feel like life isn't all that bad or bring a smile to people's faces (which I am all for), but all too often it's at the expense of something else. Case in point the Man Cave ones, which are all just useless and offensive brain drivel from some tool who needs to microphone his masculinity all over the joint, possibly not realising that it's making people feel uncomfortable more than making them laugh. Sure, *you're* tickled pink by the farting and sports and casual sexism, but there's other shit in there that kills the intended vibe. I think it's okay to want your own space or 'cave', but I don't think it needs a list of clichéd rules on the wall that you didn't even come up with yourself. Some of those are quite rough on the brains, and I'm not even a woman or non male-identifying champion who would be well within their rights to be furious reading the stupid shit on that sign. The heavy sexist stuff is a little scary and can also make other blokes feel like shit, too. The living and the laughing and the loving of sports will happen naturally because we don't need instructions.

'BEING TOLD TO "LIVE, LAUGH, LOVE" BY A PIECE OF WOOD IS NOT THE BREAKTHROUGH TIP I NEED TODAY.'

Obviously, people hang these signs probably to encourage themselves to be happier than those around them. I don't hate all positive affirmation, I just struggle with the banal ones that regurgitate the same old garbage. This lack of creativity is possibly why I imagine you don't see heaps of cheap wooden signs saying stuff like 'Fuck This Shit'.

That actually gives me an idea!

I could rebel with signs that make the offenders feel the way I do when I read their signs.

Time for negative affirmation signs!

'STRESS, PANIC, MELTDOWN'

I can see this going up above the cash register just as you go to pay and realise you're broke but have already ordered the food.

Stress Panic Meltdown

'IMPENDING DOOM'

The name of a Christian metal band, would you believe it? Anyway, this would look great over the fireplace and really highlight the flames that remind you you're going to hell.

'ALONE'

This one is in fancy wedding cake font and hangs in the toilet, reminding you that you're on your own.

'CRINGE'

I love this one. I reckon it would go so well in the dining area of someone's house that has loads of shit signs.
You can guerrilla mount it with a 3M hook that you secretly brought in your pocket.

'OH SHIT!'

Setting everyone at unease, this can literally hang anywhere you like.

'EVERYTHING SUCKS, FUCK THIS, FUCK YOU'

At last a sign I can relate to several times a day.
I would be happy to see that someone else shared the sentiment.

'JESUS, WHAT IS THAT SMELL?'

Total room killer. It will also make people sniff for trouble and have the added bonus of making the room as inviting as a man cave.

'GOOD ONE'

The sarcastic thumbs-up of signs, can be hung straight off any other shit sign.

I could do this all day. Maybe I should?

I know I've hung a stack of shit on positivity. I think being positive is great and you should definitely take it when it's there, but I don't think you should feel guilty for not having the same emotion that one of these positivity signs is dishing you. You're allowed to feel like shit sometimes and you're allowed to not listen to the decorations on the wall at a beachside café.

This may sound cruel but I'm a contrary unit, so a lot of the time when I'm around signs extolling particular vibes or outlooks, I end up feeling quite polarised by them. Maybe they send the opposite signal? Just saying.

'I WILL EXPERIENCE THE EMOTION THAT IS APPOINTED TO ME BY MY UNSTEADY BRAIN, THANK YOU VERY MUCH.'

I think you should decorate your spaces however the fucken fuck ya want, really, and if you need thirty signs telling you to digest and breathe then that's actually fine, it's just annoying for me. I'll get over it. I love taking the piss out of stuff – it's how I live, laugh and love. I think your man cave is weird, but again, you do you, matey. All I will say is: some of the sentiments on the sign you bought at the ciggie shop are a bit cooked and maybe don't represent how you truly feel about the world around you. I would ask you to reconsider and rewrite those rules to include more legends into your sick party zone. I bet it's a good time when it gets going.

I'll get off the signage horse here, but maybe this has been enough of a SIGN to take it easy on all the demanding signs, eh? It's stressing me out.

YEAH
PARTY ON
ROCK ON OR FXXKOFF!
CUT SICK
GOOD VIBES ONLY

There's nothing like an unrequested emotional cheerleader to really make any situation more difficult, and I've found this can rear its annoying head in a wide range of exhausting forms.

Deadset: since when has being told to 'Cheer up' somehow suddenly translated into actual cheer? Few phrases in the English language lack empathy as much as 'cheer up' – it truly screams 'I have no real regard for your feelings right now; in fact they are a massive inconvenience to me so if you wouldn't mind just cutting it out and feeling the way I want you to now please K THX BYE'. Yes, sure mate, you're in charge of everyone's emotions and can simply wave your shitty wand of 'cheer up' to totally sort it out. What an arrogant thing to say to someone who is having a hard time.

I believe it's fine to feel blue sometimes and not be bursting with unbridled enthusiasm 24/7. In fact, it's important to experience feelings, particularly in a safe space. Said safe space is not created by someone drop-kicking a 'cheer up' into a sad person's face.

This leads me onto the other absolute belter of shit things to say to someone who is having a rough day: 'Hey, give us a smile!' Aka probably one of the worst fucken things I've ever heard in my life, along with that heinous piece of shit commonly said to women by loser dudes:

'You'd look prettier if you smiled more.'

Oooooof, you awful poison fuckwit. If you *were* trying to be the biggest shithead on Earth I think you certainly fucken kicked the ball straight between the posts with that one, champion. I double over with cringe imagining how anyone thinks that it's an acceptable thing to say to someone. I mean, I've said some stupid shit in my life but fuck me, this horror show is next level. Offering someone unsolicited advice on how to be more attractive to you is the biggest display of up-your-own-arse deadshittery imaginable. It borders on fascinating to me that a person can exist at that level and not have some semblance of self-reflection and think *maybe that's a cooked thing to say to someone. Maybe telling a complete stranger to look hotter is super fucked and also says a lot about how great I think I am.*

From what I understand, a smile itself is a pretty simple response and it generally just happens on its own without much effort. There are some sicklord scientists out there who will tell you shit like 'You know it takes more muscles to frown than it does smile'. Which while I'm sure is true, Dr Dickhead, it's not like anyone is too exhausted to smile because they've spent all their energy frowning. Life is, believe it or not, a bit of hard work, so the occasional frown makes total and fitting sense to me, whereas smiling incessantly does not; it seems more rehearsed than it does a sign of genuine joy. Maybe I see less smiling because I live in a city and everyone here is paying too much rent and hates life 'cause they're likely on the way to a job they can't stand just to make money for someone else.

I have obviously had an issue for a long time with being told to smile. I had this 'over-smiling' game I used to play at school during the annual school photo where I thought it was super funny to try to show both rows of teeth during the command to 'smile' by the photographer. I looked like an absolute dickhead and it was worth it. It was harder to pull off in the individual portrait photo but I went for it anyway. If you look closely at my profile pic on my social media accounts where I use an old school photo of myself, you'll notice me doing it. I think by that stage my parents had accepted that I was never going to act normally in photos. Any chance to mess with a normal moment I'll take: born to be a dickhead from the start, I was.

If someone tells me to 'smile!' I am more likely to be filled with contempt for that person than deliver them the facial expression they're commanding. If they really cared, they'd ask how I was doing in earnest or else just fuck off and leave me alone. Let's be honest, they only said that 'cause they're brimming with their own sense of fulfilment like some arsehole on too many pingers at a party.

It's cool if you genuinely want to share your contentment with other people, and while a smile can be uplifting and a bit of joy can be infectious, demanding that someone smile causes the exact opposite to happen. What did you expect, by the way? Surely you'd understand that a fake smile is even worse than no smile at all? Facial expressions aren't always accurate depictions of our true emotions either, mate. Sometimes you can smile at someone and want them to fuck off all at once, therefore making the smile an untrustworthy response in general. Not every moment in the history of facial expressions has represented a person's true feelings, which are very dynamic things. Some occur out of politeness, some are the equivalent of a 'good, thanks' answer and some are from real, honest happiness. It's great to smile when you're happy but it's probably wise to remember not everyone feels the same about today as you.

For example, I've been stuck in a waiting room at a medical centre in the absolute full fucken throes of a panic attack feeling like I was gonna actually die, grabbing my chest, sitting there crying, distressed as fuck, just very visibly not great. All of a sudden a kind woman came to sit next to me. She asked if I was okay, to which I think I said something like 'I'm having a pretty bad panic attack and I feel like I'm gonna die'. She just sat with me, made sure I was actually alright and didn't even ask me to smile, would you believe it – how rude!

Actually it was the most accessible and comforting thing ever when she offered a simple check-in, one that I'll never forget. So from my experience as a first-hand unavailable smiler, maybe if you see someone feeling a little low and you truly do want to share a little genuine care for their situation, you could just ask if they are doing okay. And *not* ask them to manipulate their face, ya goose.

Then there's the phrase 'Good Vibes Only', the shaka brah of woke-signalling slogans – it too belongs to this one-size-fits-all part of the universe. From where I'm standing, it has well and truly shot itself in the foot as far as recognising that all feelings are valid, even the negative ones. Like a stamp on something that declares 'No Mental Health Problems Allowed Here', it's super demanding, entirely delusional and ultimately unrealistic. It's called toxic positivity and feels very surf shop level psychology to drill this kind of message into someone. I feel like this sign is pointing at you in judgement and reporting on everyone's wellness status: 'Oi, you there! Feel good or else be a fucken loser.'

I think the 'Good Vibes Only' phrase is *trying* to tick the 'Don't Be A Dickhead' box, which I am on board with, but it's a little too 'Don't have a bad one!' to set anyone at ease. If I see it on a sign somewhere, I am instantly annoyed because my brain sees 'GOOD ONLY' and knows it's absolute bullshit. There's no way you can enforce this shit. If there were, I imagine it would go down a little like this:

> 'Excuse me there, bro, are your vibes *good*? Everyone else's vibes are *very* good so yours also better be *very* good, otherwise we will have to use *bad* vibes to eject your bad vibes from the *good* vibes area, and therefore remove ourselves for having the incorrect vibes . . . Hang on? OH GOD NOOOOO!'*

See! Doesn't work.

So I do kinda understand what GVO is trying to achieve, but I think we can agree it's doing a shit job of it. To the regular person with mental health problems, I see this slogan and mindset to be more of a threat and judgement than a positive thing. Getting happy takes work and needs a lot of environmental support. Ya can't just chuck a sick drive-by and throw the *Good Vibes Gazette* at my head expecting life to get better. Ya gotta care for yourself, do right by yourself, be kind, set boundaries

---

* insert explosion.

and take space from shitheads. Ignoring shit throwaway lifestyle suggestions is a good thing to add to your arsenal.

Getting happy is such a huge focus for so many and it's the mission impossible we might not ever fully complete – and that's okay. It's a big ask. Throw on top all the events, people, relationships, jobs, fuckheads, injuries and general malaise life entails and your chances are looking a little hairy.

There are a lot of schools of thought as to what happiness really is. Is it just dopamine? Is it the feeling of contentment? Is it just not feeling like miserable shit all the time?

Remember that happiness is relative to the individual, and the expectation of it to happen can often give you the shits more than help get you actually there. It seems like the holy grail of emotions, this unobtainable, shiny thing that means all-you-can-eat smiles and never-ending good times.

As someone who was raised a Christian for the first half of my life, I was taught the concept of eternal joy and eternal life, but informed they'd only be enjoyed by those who were very well-behaved and made it to heaven. It sounded sick at the time, the true GVO place. I mean, how fucken wild would it be to hang in a joint where everything was perfect and no one ever got sick or felt bad and you had everything you ever dreamed of and all your mates were there . . . except the ones who didn't get in 'cause they weren't Christians but were still amazing people, or maybe they were someone whose life was really tough, maybe so awful that they took their own life. Well, sadly the Bible says that if you take your own life then you can't get into heaven, sorry.

My young brain found the promise of eternal joy pretty confusing, as there are a lot of holes in the concept if so many people are excluded from it. Eternal joy and happiness actually sound fucking exhausting. I reckon even in heaven you'd still have people asking, 'How ya going?', which to be fair would be a waste of time since everything's obviously doing great up there, don't ya know?

Last time I checked, happiness and joy aren't the only emotions that make us feel complete as humans. As much as I'm not actively seeking out a reason to cry, it's actually kind of cathartic to have a good cry and feel out what you're going through every now and then. The idea of being somewhere where no one cries or feels low or writes a sad song or watches a sad movie, well that is a massive bummer to me. Fuck, that would get old fast, though maybe I wouldn't care that it got old because I'd be so happy about things getting old, right? 'Oh god, this unstoppable joy is relentless but so . . . great.' It all seems bizarre. Taking the big-hitter emotions like heartbreak, sadness and even anger out of existence seems very strange and not what would in the end actually make you feel authentically whole.

What if happiness comes from a sense of really

experiencing the full highs and lows of our existence, and manifests in lots of less obvious ways than 'Good Vibes Only' t-shirts and dickheads commanding us to cheer up? I dunno, I'm not a fucken wellness expert and nor do I feel like becoming one any time soon, but I am someone who has struggled to find the positivity in my day most days of my life and knows what it's like to feel the relief of an actual moment of joy. I know what happiness feels like to me and that's all I can comment on – your happiness might look very bloody different to mine or to that of the person who has a bumper sticker telling you what to feel. Happiness in all its manifestations is out there somewhere and probably not inside a place with a fucken neon sign giving you a tan with its cringey bullshit. Then again, maybe it is. Maybe you're not a massive pessimist like me and seeing these signs makes you feel a little joy – and that's okay too.

'LAST TIME I CHECKED, HAPPINESS AND JOY AREN'T THE ONLY EMOTIONS THAT MAKE US FEEL COMPLETE AS HUMANS.'

MY POEM ABOUT GOOD VIBES ONLY

I see you in the bar window
Shining so bright

With a seeming list of demands
For entry tonight.

This super cool bar
Ain't for no phoneys
With a sign out front that says:

Good
Vibes
Only!

Those are the rules
This is the law
I'd love a quiet drink
But I'm not so sure
That my vibe is quite right

For this fancy bar
I've had a tough day
I even cried in my car.

Maybe that will all change?
If I go inside
Or will I be found out
By its watchful eye?

Too bad!
Piss off!

Says the neon sign

LIFE: WHAT NAT TO DO

You are not welcome here
With your incorrect vibe.

Go clean yourself up
And bring back better

Something to match the clientele
And the other trend-setters.

For this is a bar where
No one is sad or lonely

This is a bar where we have

Good
Vibes
Only!

I don't think we have to win a gold medal every day to feel
okay or even happy; sometimes 'just okay' is pretty good.
I have had a lot of Barry Crockers of days when everything
seemed to be fucken doomed to sadness and depression,
as if that was the point of life. Then someone gave me a big
long hug as I cried a big deep cry for an hour or more in
their arms. Afterwards something weird happened where
we smiled and laughed 'cause I realised in that moment that
everything is probably okay – but also kinda probably still
gonna be shit again, lol.

We give ourselves such a fucken hard time to be stuff
for everyone: 'be happy', 'be well', 'stay positive'. But ironing

on a smile can take a fucken back seat and shut the fuck up for a hot sec while I muscle through my dogshit day, thanks very much. I once spent an entire Tuesday being yelled at by a random arsehole while I packed a truck with bullshit and drove it around town with no air con in the middle of summer only to be yelled at again by another rando dickhead because of something that had nothing to do with me. After that type of Grade-A nonsense, maybe if I'm lucky I'll kick back with my best mate and have a big old plate of Viennetta ice cream 'cause I can't believe they still make that stuff and we reckon it would be funny to buy it for a laugh, then we'll proceed to have way too much as today can get in the fucken bin. We'll sit on the couch and laugh 'til we can't breathe, and in that moment I'll feel a sense of huge relief and . . . happy?

Does that count? Is that good enough to be called happy? Am I happy 'cause I experienced a happy moment? Would that happy moment even have happened if I didn't have a shit time dealing with unhappy things earlier? All I know is, that's the moment that makes it okay for me right then. Maybe tomorrow will have fewer fuckwits in it? Maybe not.

I can most certainly say that 'Good vibes are rad, yet shit also happens' is probably more accurate, and a little more kind to the mind of an anxious person, though it may require a longer bumper to fit the sticker version on. I will probably smile later, but not because some up-themselves hero told me to; it's probably because I'm telling my mate about the tool who told me to, and laughing about it.

As for 'Cheer up' . . . sure, provided you 'Get sad now, please'.

Go be sad, go be happy, go be whatever the fuck ya want and while you're at it, let other people do the same.

'Complex Vibes Only.'

I've always been fascinated by people who can just switch gears in life and give it all up to lead a seemingly happier, simpler existence. Like the optimist who throws caution and possibly safer decisions in the bin as they sell all their shit and live in a van or travel around swapping work for board and meals etc. I mean, what's the worst that could happen?

For a while I had this fantasy of becoming a hippie and moving into some kind of pain-in-the-arse van or commune where the whole fucken vibe was all very untouchably chill, everyone and everything just got along, I never wore shoes and used that crystal deodorant that doesn't work. As I've grown older I've realised that what my idea of a hippie is and what a hippie is *actually* like these days are two very different things. After going to enough techno festivals in the bush and sitting around drum circles with people chewing their faces off, I'm certain that becoming a hippie would probably be a bad move for me, since there is only so much psytrance and contact juggling I can take before I lose my mind.

I think I've put the 1960s and 70s hippie set-up on a pedestal more than today's offering – back when everyone listened to multiple bands with multiple members in them and smoked weed that didn't send them to hospital in a panic. The shit part about getting older is that I've become much more pragmatic and have reconciled myself to the fact that me embracing total hippiedom isn't super realistic.

While it is technically possible for me to throw the towel in and become a hippie, buy a Kombi and park up somewhere by the ocean, the cost alone would be monumental. My logistical mind has pulled apart this scenario a thousand times over and has sapped it of all the fun.

This is how I see the idealised hippie life move going down and why it won't likely go well for me:

As a hippie, it's very important to me that I'm giving off a properly convincing laid-back image. I need the right visual cues to help convey that I have made a radical life-changing shift to a more carefree lifestyle. I have a few things on my side that will make some of this change easy, but other parts of my existence will have quite the opposite effect. I have the 'long hair don't care' vibe going already and my nose pierced, so I'm off to the races in that department. While it's a classic hippie look, I don't believe it's a prerequisite, so really it's just an added bonus to help bullshit everyone around me into thinking that I'm chilled out now. I do play guitar and drums and I do also occasionally dabble in writing shit poetry (as demonstrated on page 28), so that will work in my favour when it comes to evenings spent sitting around the old camp fire, I imagine.

But while I know the #VanLyf thing is very common in hippie circles, the issue here is that currently I drive a very loud 90's model Subaru, and while it *is* an all-wheel drive that would be great for taking it off road a little, it does boast a massive cannon exhaust so if I parked at a camp site it would shit everyone to tears and I would likely be asked to leave immediately . . . not very laid-back.

In my mind, the hippie look always has the classic Volkswagen Kombi van attached to it. These things are not fucken cheap these days, or easy to source, either – a vintage one is around fifty years old and any decent vehicle will fetch ya a bill of well over $40,000: that's a very stressful amount of money. At the moment my life is pretty fucken stressful as it is, which isn't something I enjoy about it, to be honest. From what I understand about the hippie lifestyle, stress is not a welcome attribute, so I would need to give up the stressful aspects of my life. To me, buying a fifty-year-old German van that has no radiator or air con for driving around in the Australian heat doesn't seem at all like a fucken smart or stress-lowering move.

I realise there's joy to be found in driving an old car that needs a bit of love, but come on, these things can fucken catch fire, mate. I've seen it happen on the side of the freeway with my own eyes. If I'm going to begin to chill out in life, then the worst thing that could happen would be for everything I own to go up in flames in the back of a stylish but decrepit Kombi.

This is not looking good.

I have lived in *a lot* of share houses and unusual living spaces in my time. Some of the amenities in said living spaces have been fairly rough and ready, to say the least. I have showered in cupboards, cooked over camp stoves indoors, slept in a tent in my lounge room, kipped on a bed made from couch cushions, had mice and/or cockroaches run up the back of my t-shirt while asleep at night, not washed my clothes for six months, peed into bottles and overall lived quite a fucken chat lifestyle in the past. I'm no stranger to being a real grub, but this is not something I am proud of or a way of life I want to embrace anymore. This could very much pose a problem with my new #VanLyfstyle. Hitting the road and leaving all my responsibilities behind is supposed to be a step forwards, not backwards.

I did once give #VanLyf a brief shot with my best mate Austin on a trip north. It was pretty great for a hot second but some shit got old quickly. The trouble showering, for one. I love a good shower, but not in the ocean with dishwashing detergent (don't worry, it was the eco brand one so don't call the EPA on me). I thought I was being quite industrious at the time, telling myself, *It's all soap, it's all the same shit* . . . wrong. I gave it a shot at Burleigh Heads one morning, took the bottle into the ocean and tried to wash myself. It was so fucked, it wouldn't wash off and just left me slippery and greasy. One of the reasons I couldn't get it off my body may have been because I was washing myself in salt water. What a shitshow! I'm sure there is a soap expert out there dying inside, just waiting to rinse me (lol) over using dish detergent to wash my human skin, but hey, at least I tried to clean myself.

I should also mention that sleeping in a hot van when I already have sleeping issues is quite the opposite of chill, so that is gonna throw another spanner in the works.

Another aspect of the hippie dream I think I may struggle with is fire twirling. After what might happen in my Kombi van, I have a fear of fire so this is going to stress me out.

'I WANT TO BE ABLE TO JUST LET IT ALL GO AND TWIRL AROUND LIKE A DICKHEAD WITHOUT A CARE IN THE WORLD.'

Plus, at the time of writing, we're still being advised to not meet in large groups, and I know that my commune is gonna have several large groups. Imagine the hugging and the coughing and the— Nah, I'm out.

What I really want is to be more relaxed about life in general. Although the facade of a relaxed lifestyle seems great, it lacks some of the unrelaxing things that I enjoy, like death metal, loud cars, video games, making lots of noise and swearing heaps. I do respect the bravery or naivety that it takes to be laid back and trust in the universe to look after you. I always loved the happy-go-lucky characters in movies I watched growing up too, from Pauly Shore in *Bio-Dome* and Lori Petty in *Tank Girl* to The Dude in one of my favourite movies, *The Big Lebowski*. I loved how no matter what the fuck these characters were faced with they were always like, 'Fuck it, it's all good'. I found enormous comfort in watching characters like this because it's literally the fucken opposite of what my brain does when faced with drama.

'LEAVING IT ALL BEHIND AND DIVING HEADFIRST INTO HAPPY-GO-LUCKY IS SCARY SHIT.'

I want to be able to just let it all go and twirl around like a dickhead without a care in the world, but the truth is I can't and likely won't, because I'm me. I'm someone with anxiety and a history of overthinking everything. I have a brain that needs me to hyper-analyse everything all the time and act accordingly.

When presented with a 'what's the worst that could happen?' scenario, it's like someone hires Hollywood in my brain and pumps out endless blockbuster movies where I make myself the loser piece of shit character who needs to go down at the end of every one.

This is why I'd make a shit hippie; I would analyse everything way too much and ruin the coastal chill vibe. I've already established that I would be sleep-deprived, dirty, on fire in a van and would have caught several illnesses from group hugs in a commune, and that's just the beginning of me pulling this apart. I am fascinated by anything that signals itself as overly meaningful. It wouldn't take long for someone to read me some fucken shit poem or put on some performance to whale song and I would end up panic laughing 'cause I was uncomfortable and end up getting in trouble. Shortly afterwards I would no doubt feel so awful for finding it that funny and would end up apologising and trying to backpedal with some story that they didn't care about because they just want me to fuck off now. Trying to fit into a laid-back lifestyle would just plant me forever in a state of endless apology and self-doubt. I'm not built for it. Leaving it all behind and diving headfirst into happy-go-lucky is scary shit and could end badly. My dad has told me never to move to the place you go on holidays and it was for this reason, I think. I mean, worse things happen than moving somewhere new and giving it a shot, I suppose, but for me the stakes are high for a monumental fuck-up.

'TRYING TO FIT INTO A LAID-BACK LIFESTYLE WOULD JUST PLANT ME FOREVER IN A STATE OF ENDLESS APOLOGY AND SELF-DOUBT.'

I often don't need to go anywhere to have imagined what would go wrong for me there. It's anxiety and all its mighty strength at work; it makes all the safe stuff, unsafe . . . all the calm, unsettled. The worst that can happen is often already playing out in my head and won't allow for other realities or possibilities to get involved. It manifests in all sorts of nonstop entertainment – it's never not fucking annoying, to be perfectly honest. It wastes so much of my life, making me sit there shitting myself over things that haven't even happened, but my brain can't get enough. I love to tell myself why things won't work out because I don't believe I deserve them. I think I deserve to be punished for every mistake I've made in my life and that social anxiety, self-doubt and endless stress is my punishment.

If it is in fact my punishment then it's a fucking brutal one. It punishes me all the time, every day. I often sit across from people and convince myself they hate me because of my body language or because of the way I said something – it's brutal. The other person most likely has no idea what the fuck I'm talking about when I eventually crumble into awkwardness and bring it up. Sometimes I just don't say anything and decide that this is the way the movie ends; I have cast them in their role without them even knowing and made myself the shithead everyone hates again. I can go years without saying things to some people because I've already lived out the worst that can happen in the situation without it even being real or them knowing. I am scared of some old friendships I've let fall by the wayside because we had a difference of opinion years ago and now I'm convinced they'd have no reason to like me anymore. Even though we had more or less worked it out, I've decided they've changed their mind.

A few months ago I went into my local corner store and grabbed a drink from the fridge only to find out they'd been robbed of some cash moments earlier. The person behind the counter was in distress, understandably, and said something like 'Someone just took the cash from the back of the store and ran off'. I asked if they saw what the thief looked like. 'They were wearing a hat,' they replied. I was a bit lost in that moment, not knowing how to help, seeing that people were already on the phone, likely to the cops. It was anxiety central. I put my drink back and left the store, thinking I was just adding more anxious energy and there were lots of people there already onto it. I went back the next day and asked how it was going and if it was resolved, and the person behind the counter gave me what looked like a disapproving frown. Within a split second I thought *I bet they think it was me, I had a hat on . . . OMG*, then proceeded to go home shitting the gear and had to be talked down from a really hectic panic that I was a suspect in a robbery.

I think becoming a hippie for me is a complicated and risky escapist dreamland, and while I do value a good bloody daydream about an easier way of life and do think it's a positive thing to have a place to go in your head when times are tough, the reality of it is probably hugely stressful and a dream best left in my imagination where I can manage the possible oops. It looks real pretty being all smiles and sunshine but that's not really me. My reality is much more complex. At the moment I need a radiator, I need a loud exhaust, I enjoy a touch of timely air con, and maybe I need to have awkward conversations and make myself a suspect in robberies I wasn't a part of just to crack jokes about it?

Who the fuck knows? I tell ya what, by the time I have figured it out, you better believe I still won't be investing in a fifty-year-old van and pretending I'm not scared of it catching fire.

KEEP YOUR FRIENDS CLOSE AND YOUR ENEMIES CLOSER

Ease up, *Game of Thrones*, it's not medieval times anymore, nor are you ever going to use that cheap ninja sword you bought from the markets to defend anything except yourself from your own shadow.

When I was in my teens, I remember meeting some dickhead hardarse who had brought a massive Bowie knife with him to a party just to show people how tough he was. I'm pretty sure he had sunnies on at night, too, which is usually a red flag, in my experience. When I asked why he was kitted up like Rambo, I'm pretty sure he had a rather distressing answer to do with dealing with his enemies or some shit I won't repeat, but which I also heavily suspect was total bullshit. Let's just say I don't think anyone really thought it was cool; pretty sure everyone thought he was a fucken gronk. Hugely unsettling to be around, the poor kid needed some help, better role models, better mates or to feel validated in some way other than carrying a fucken massive weapon on him. I hope he worked his way through all those issues.

I reflect on moments from when I was a kid, like going to the cinema to watch shit like *Batman*, a super badass movie with a main character who kicked the arse of anyone who messed with him. I didn't have a lot of mates at that time and tended to be picked on, and I also didn't have a super happy home life either, so daydreaming that I had bat wings and a 'Ya don't wanna mess with this cool dude' attitude was a nice thing to believe was real. I may not have had a great deal of friends back then, but I sure as hell wasn't going to let any enemies (imagined or real) win, at least in my mind.

Watching epic, loud movies in dark cinemas felt super empowering, particularly to see someone refusing to take shit from nobody. I left the cinema feeling like an absolute hero after that. It even changed the way I walked: a couple of fists down by my sides, bottom lip bitten, struttin' like this ten-year-old Dark Knight filled with sugar-covered cola bottle lollies who you sure didn't want to mess with. It was as if I had just watched some sort of training video.

I imagine what it must be like to be a parent in these moments when your kid transforms into a candy-filled superhero in front of your eyes – probably both hilarious and annoying all at once. How funny to see your little darling sitting in the back seat of the car on the way home, arms crossed and all tough now, saying shit like 'Don't mess with me, guys, okay?' and your response being to laugh, before getting in trouble for laughing. All of that facade maintained until you arrive at McDonald's and they have to break character to order what they want for dinner.

'What do you wanna eat, Batman?'

'Happy Meal with nuggets . . . Please . . . AND DON'T FORGET THE TOY.'

Very tough dinner choice, phwoar.

Fuck, *The Matrix* really did a number on my young brain too. It was the perfect set-up for an out-of-place kid. All you had to do was swallow a blue tablet, sit on a chair with a plug in ya head connected to a computer and you became a kung fu master – it was that quick, what a ripper! Knowing any martial arts as a youngster was always a huge flex. I reckon back then I was spending many a post-school afternoon sitting back in chairs attempting to plug my head in to the family Pentium with a cable from behind the television, trying to download movie-quality moves into my head, probably convincing myself that I had, too. That would, I imagine, be followed by going out to the backyard with a stick and twirling it around like a fucken drunk hippy at a doof. I remember pulling lots of 'crane' stances as well. The stances, OMG – so much action went on in the bathroom mirror thinking I was looking at a dangerous man, shadow-boxing with my reflection and shit. You didn't want to mess with Nathaniel. *

All of this for the most part is very sweet and harmless but I do think a little guidance and love is needed in the background to help shape a person so they won't go on to feel the need to imitate The Joker as a grown-up.

---

* insert karate chop hands.

Just about all of us, I reckon, did cringey shit when we were youngsters just trying to feel seen and heard. When the whole world doesn't make any fucken sense and you kinda don't fit in anywhere, it's hard to know how to behave or what to do about it. Some of the awkward stuff I did as a young person makes me want to double over with panic and embarrassment – and, god, to be that young again would be an absolute ultimate punishment for me. Fucken hell, good thing we only age in one direction.

But hey, let's have a geez at this saying 'keep your friends close and enemies closer'. It seems obvious to me that keeping your friends close is a great idea, but in terms of keeping enemies closer, that's maybe a shit idea. It sounds like, 'let's have very few boundaries', which is a risky move.

Who has actual enemies as an adult anyway? It's not fucken Batman and The Joker we're talking about, it's the real world where it's probably closer to Steven and Craig who are struggling to see eye to eye.

Let's say, for argument's sake, Craig – sorry if your name is Craig and you're reading this, by the way – is becoming a really draining human for Steven to be around. He doesn't make Steven feel particularly heard or seen and it looks like it's become time to do things as separate humans. Great call in my eyes, fucken absolutely let each other go; maybe some other people can hold more space for Craig's behaviour. But Steven isn't one of those people right now, simply because it makes him feel like shit.

He shouldn't keep Craig around just to suffer his company; it's not fair on either of them.

No one is your real enemy unless you're at war, and even then it's sometimes ambiguous. We are taught to see things in these extreme terms, whereby someone is either with you or against you. People can have different priorities and desires from each other and that's pretty normal as far as I can tell. There's a bucketload of reality TV shows and media out there that tries to program ya head to see people's different ways of experiencing the world as the makings of a conflict. They produce these over-dramatised situations that may very well not have been necessary or even real. Not all interactions in life are filled with drama and nor should they be. It's fine to love seeing a bit of drama that's not yours, but saying it's 'reality' is taking the piss.

Sometimes we don't get along, that's very standard-issue real-life stuff. We don't all like the same shit and if we did it would be a pain in the arse. Look at the PlayStation 5 issue for example. Too many people liked it at the same time and so they fucken ran out of them, and now you have to buy one off some dickhead in a car park who has acquired fifteen of the fuckers and is charging people heaps more than the original price for it. (This may or may not have happened to me.) My point is that having diverse tastes and ways of thinking is actually pretty good, and it doesn't have to turn into fucken World War III all the time.

Just because you don't like someone doesn't make them

your enemy; it makes them more of a pain in the arse, and we all deal with pains in the arse daily. If you want actual enemies, play a video game where you can live out that fantasy safely.

Admittedly, there is a small rectangular hole in my story where I have, in fact, kept an enemy of mine very close and in the process it has become quite a good friend: The Tucka Fucka.

My microwave is named this because of its innate ability to fuck up tucker (funnily enough not what it was designed for). I have a complex and bizarre relationship with the Tucka Fucka. (I should mention why it is spelled this way and not Tuck*er* Fuck*er*. I wanted to plaster the name of it on the front of the microwave's door and when I got to the hardware shop to buy the stick-on letters they'd run out of 'e' and 'r', so Tuck*a* Fuck*a* it is.) I have become quite obsessed with it, though not for the reasons you might think. I don't actually cook food in it to enjoy, but it does make me laugh how ridiculous a merry-go-round of a device it can be.

The obsession has got mildly out of hand, to the point where I have started collecting vintage microwave cookbooks; I even have fans of my YouTube channel send them to me, which is very lovely. I must have at least thirty now, and the recipes in them are nothing short of take-your-breath-away hilarious. I get such a huge laugh out of the disgusting and dated recipes in these books and want to try to make them all (a few of these attempts are on my channel).

FRIGHTENING MICROWAVE RECIPES

Melon and Ham Pasta Salad

Absolutely as frightening as it sounds, and I've fucken eaten it on camera to prove it. Whoever thought melon and creamy pasta went together needs to hear the word 'no' more often.

Microwave Roast Chicken

Seriously? The whole fucking chicken goes in the microwave for 45 minutes!!! And because it doesn't really go brown, you cover the skin in powdered onion soup, which is known in the microwaving world as a 'browning agent'. Fuck that.

Angels on Horseback (Microwaved Oysters)

Wrap ya brains around this puke circus: bacon and oysters skewered together and then decimated in the microwave for 9 minutes, served on toast and then garnished with the world's most underwhelming ingredient – watercress. I don't know what gave the ratbag who came up with this recipe the vision of an angel that rides a horse. To me it's closer to a goblin riding a turd.

> **Escargots with Garlic Butter (Microwaved Snails)**
>
> I don't know if you can get locked up for cooking heinous food, but if you could, this dish would shoot you to the back of a cop car so fast you wouldn't know what hit ya. This concoction promises it's 'an ideal starter for your gourmet friends'. I don't reckon you would have any mates left if you served them twenty-four 'canned snails' that had been warmed up in the Tucka Fucka. Seriously no idea how anyone on Earth could eat this.

Cooking a dish from an old-school microwave cookbook became a part of my live shows, because those laughs needed to be shared. I have toured the country with a fucken microwave, and let me tell you, it is the shittest idea I've ever had.

No one wants anything to do with it. When I try to check it in at the airport, the staff are like, 'LOL, what?' Uber drivers don't want to take it in their vehicle even though it easily fits in the boot of their car, so keeping this enemy close has made my tours incredibly hard at times. The amount it has cost to transport a microwave around the country is fucking absurd. It has cost me about ten times the price of the fucken thing in the first place, but I love it. I love it because it makes me and other people laugh.

I was originally going to tour with the microwave that Jules and I have at home, which I picked up for about $25 at some old knick-knack shed sale thing, but just before we left to go on tour the Tucka Fucka started to turn on whenever you *opened* the door. Terrifying. Now, I'm not sure how the radiation aspect of microwaves works, but I'm pretty certain it's not supposed to be activated while the door is open. I had to get it tested and tagged for the tour and was pretty sure having it switch on with the door open was gonna halt proceedings, not to mention how much it would scare the shit out of the audience, and frightening the crowd is not really the vibe I'm chasing at my shows.

Anyway, I ended up buying a new one so I didn't have the damn thing radiating the front row at the shows, which means now I have TWO.

Two enemies. The best enemies I've ever had.

Funny how that relationship changed over time. Even though it is an inanimate object, I have this strange affection for it because it has made me laugh so much. Am I laughing at it or with it? At it, of course! But it's a Tucka Fucka and it's okay to laugh at it.

'I'M SURE THERE ARE A FEW PEOPLE OUT THERE WHO HAVE HAD ENOUGH OF MY CARRY-ON OVER THE YEARS.'

When it comes to people, I think if you don't like someone anymore, that's okay. They don't have to become your enemy, though – you can just set up some good old boundaries. Boundaries are great for saying, 'Nup, not into that shit. You do you over there and I'll be elsewhere, cheers.'

Life goes on and people change. Some people change into fuckwits, which sucks, but hey. It's a bummer, but is objectively only your opinion of them (which is valid), and whether or not that corresponds to the view they have of themselves, at the end of the day no one is making you bloody hang out with them, right? If they are going to a party and you also want to attend, you can analyse those boundaries and decide whether you're comfortable being in the same place with them and if that's gonna be a safe move for you. If it's a staunch boundary, go do other shit. They are dynamic things, boundaries, and can work however you want them to, as long as they're yours. You should respect other people's, of course, so that we all get to choose what we want to do and with whom.

If you realise *you* have become the enemy, then it'll be time to hang out somewhere else for a while, maybe reflect on your shit and talk to some people to see if you were being a gronk after all. Either way, the oyster is your world and you shouldn't have to keep hanging around people you don't want to see or at least in a way you don't like, especially if they're being shitheads.

I'm sure there are a few people out there who have had enough of my carry-on over the years. I've been a dickhead plenty of times and have needed to work on that shit in the past, which has definitely entailed setting up a few boundaries around my own nonsense.

With all that said, I think we should refresh and modernise the saying 'keep your friends close and your enemies closer' to something much more relevant to now. Here are a few alternatives I'd like to throw into the ring:

1. Keep your friends close and that will be just great.
2. Microwave your enemies' lunch.
3. Set up boundaries around dickheads.
4. If they have sunnies on and a knife, hand them a mirror and run.
5. Reality TV isn't real.
6. Party, or don't.
7. Keep your enemies in video games and your PlayStation closer.
8. Not everyone is everyone's mate.
9. Stop regurgitating shit old sayings, Nat.
10. 💩

MAN
UP

Where to start with this cripplingly dated gem of gendered advice? Man up, eh? Man up where? Like, upwards? Over them mountains? Into the back garage? Like 'Up The Mighty Tigeeeeerrrs'? I'm confused, and not only because I obviously know what you're trying to say to me, but also because as an apparent 'man' myself, though I often struggle to identify with my own kind, I am truly lost when someone says 'Man up' to me.

Wherever you look, the dictionary definition of 'Man up' is consistently a version of:

> **To be brave or tough enough to deal with a difficult or unpleasant situation, eg 'You just have to man up and take it'.**

So whenever I'm told by some tough unit to man up, as a male apparently that means I need to embrace my job as a man to be tough and brave in the face of difficult unpleasantness. Well, wasn't *that* incredibly helpful. I hadn't thought of that, cheers. But what about when someone who isn't male or doesn't identify as male is faced with unpleasantness or a difficult situation, what are they supposed to do? Man up too? That may end up being quite insulting, I imagine.

This ridiculous fucking gendered saying is so tired and useless that not only does it make zero sense, but I'm willing to bet that for most people it doesn't even actually help deal with any of the aforementioned unpleasantness or difficult situations. In fact, I suspect quite the opposite.

From where I'm sitting as a male, I see the person voicing their suggestion to 'Man up' as very uncreative, lost for words, uncompassionate and on some strange recruitment drive to collect more men like themselves. Telling another man to be more like their idea of a man is bent right out of shape, let me tell ya. That shit is broken and bizarre and pretty self-involved. It is a thinly veiled effort dressed up as an encouraging cliché to try to fill the 'lesser man' with more courage and support, but in reality it just ends up more like a bit of:

> **'Aren't ya tuff eNuff brOOOooo?'**
> **'Can't you handle this shit?'**
> **'Are you weak, are ya?'**

It reads much more that way to me than as any genuine encouragement to 'hang in there' in the face of a tough situation. What if I'm being bullied at work? Just man up and damage my mental health and general wellbeing by silently suffering a frightening person? Great call! Maybe I don't have enough money to pay my rent because life – no problem, champ, just MAN UP, leave the house and go rob a bank with your unstoppable manliness. See how easy that was?

WORST MAN-BRANDED PRODUCTS

Mansize Meals

Whoever the gender genius was that decided no other genders would be able to muscle down a mighty frozen meal weighing 500 g was possibly accidentally doing them a favour by drawing them away from its foul-flavoured presence. Not only is it ridiculous to suggest that some meals are for men only, it's also pretty boring.

Just for Men

It's fucken hair dye . . . come on now. I actually made a skit video about this once by pretending to give Jules Just for Men to see what the consequences would be if a woman used it. I edited the video to include several explosions and suitable fake chaos.

Manwich

Much like the first one, it's a sandwich apparently for men only and I hate it, thanks.

Mansize Tissues

Since when do men need a fucken beach towel to blow their noses? Your nose is not special, it's just a nose like everyone else's. I'm sure it's great at smelling barbecues and 2-stroke oil but it doesn't need bigger tissues.

Men's Razors

They are cheaper for some strange reason but do the very same shit as women's razors. Go figure. The thing that shits me is not that men's razors are directed at men only but that women get taxed for using products that do the very same thing. Fuck that, get in the bin.

Man Bags

It's actually just a bag and yes, you may be a man but the two don't need to be said together for it to be what it already is. Isn't it a little strange that many other 'man' products are about being a larger size, but not the man bag? I wonder if its smallness supposedly emasculates the owner, hence the need to inject more masculinity into its name to compensate. Heads up: the smallness doesn't necessitate a gender reveal party.

Us blokes are held hostage by stupid, dated ideologies of how we are supposed to act in situations of struggle, how our emotions are meant to come across and how our so-called manliness will be ranked as result of all of that.

Do we only become true men once we have in fact manned up? Did we 'man' good enough to the other men? Did you totally crush the other man's hand when you shook it? 'Cause if you didn't squeeze it so hard it left their ring imprinted in their flesh for three days, then maybe you're not the man you thought you were.

While we are on this subject, can we just take a moment to talk this one out?

We are told so often that a firm handshake is oh so *very* important. Apparently it's a sign of respect and all sorts of bizarre shit blah blah blah. God forbid you don't feel like touching someone immediately after meeting them, or even that you have a sore hand. 'DON'T BE A WUSS, SHAKE MY HAND!' Nah, I'll be right, thanks.

Not enough is said about the almightily unnecessary power-grip handshake. Can we pleeeeeeeease fucking stop this weird performative handshake behaviour? Staring the other person down while delivering a vicious bone-breaking FIRM HANDSHAKE that almost rips my fucking hand off while you power-announce your name: 'Peter, mate'. Yo, it's super fucking annoying, and oi . . . it hurts, hey.

Do you want to win the handshake? Is that what all this macho posturing is about?

Are you trying to scare me into thinking you're stronger than me? What is actually going on here? Are you so lost in your sense of yourself that you need to hurt the person you're greeting while simultaneously broadcasting your own name at them? Forget winning – I'm afraid it's not winning anyone over, that one. The only thing you're going to establish after an interaction where you look someone in the eyes, grab them by the hand, say your name at them and then cause a profound amount of physical pain is 'I'm a super aggressive fuckwit'. I get that you have breathtaking grip strength and may it forever be congratulated at your rock climbing gym, but in the real world most people don't enjoy having the twenty-seven bones in their hand pancaked together while the names of other people are yelled at them.

Just so you know, there is a literal contest out there called the Strongman Competition that is an event created for people to impress others with their strength in a much more consensual way than you shattering my metacarpals. The fact that these events are still called strong*man* may imply they need a bit of workshopping, since people of other genders compete in them these days, but nonetheless it's a better place to flex than during a greeting so maybe go sign up for that, champion.

To me this super macho handshake is more a sign of insecurity than a sign of respect, or whatever the supposed point of it is. I'm sure, very truly, that you're impressive in many other parts of your life outside of breaking hands and being intense to meet. I just think the idea a firm manly handshake is going to form a memorable and positive first impression of you is odd – a smile and a hello is pretty tried and true, just saying. PS Have we learnt nothing from this COVID adventure? You don't need to touch people to say hello; in fact it's been proven to make you less sick if you don't. Though I have noticed myself throwing out the classic new model elbow bump or short-distance wave to avoid handshakes this past while and that also seems weird. I can't sit here microphoning about aggressive handshakes while throwing elbows like some Muay Thai wannabe, as that might not send a great message either? Hmmm, a lot to unpack.

Anyway, I digest ;)

The firm handshake is the tip of the iceberg of stupid garbage you're told as a bloke that you need to master to gain the respect of others. It's shitty, outdated and can get in the bin along with being a stoic brick wall.

Don't be weird, dude – people love you for who you are, not for your 2000-psi handshake.

The whole what-it-is-to-be-a-real-man conundrum is complex for someone like me who's struggled with my relationship to masculinity a lot of my life. While I am definitely a masculine-presenting man and have a lot of very blokey mannerisms, I am also quite feminine in other ways and I really like that about myself. I have a mixture of desires as a man to be certain things, some of them very

cliché man traits like being big and strong, yet I also
hold close to me the other parts of who I am that can be
tender and caring. I love buying and being given flowers
for example, wearing eyeliner and listening to sad music,
as well as other traditionally so-called girly stuff that I'm
apparently not supposed to like as a man.

I have often been considered a little androgynous by
a lot of people. In fact, much is said about the way I look,
particularly on social media, with a great deal of 'is this a
girl or a guy?' commentary, or super ignorant deadshit stuff
such as 'this chick has a pretty deep voice', but hey, guess
what? I dig that about myself. I experienced a lot of similar
stuff as a teenager too, when I had long hair and travelled to
some parts of the world where people would talk to me as if
I were female, asking my dad if he and his 'daughter' were
looking for a cab etc. It was an interesting experience, don't

get me wrong, but in hindsight not one that bothered me a great deal. I think a small part of me was spun out about it, but I was young and still learning a lot about the universe. I liked the idea that no one knew my gender in those moments – maybe because that was my chance to not act like a man for second, which was kinda liberating.

I have been exposed to no shortage of bizarre displays of what I was supposed to aspire to be as a fella. Growing up, my representations of what a man was came from films and TV shows filled with big, loud blokes saving the world from itself, fighting and shooting people. In everything from TV ads for fucken barbecues and power tools to even kids' cartoons featuring cringey characters whose advances towards women were flat-out terrifying, real men were consistently conquerors of all the bad stuff and rescuers of women. When you're young and trying to work out how to behave, there's no shortage of rapid-fire toxic messaging coming from all angles – and it's fucken heavy. And just so I don't sound too 'men's rights!' and 'how hard us blokes have had it', I want to give a solid nod to the tidal wave of lethal stuff that young women are told to be, particularly when it's by men – so fucken gross and uncool.

Young people's brains are like sponges that soak up any info from around them, so when you're fed a heavy dose of gendered demands like 'man up' or its female equivalent, 'smile more' (see page 19), it makes knowing what to become as a person in general very confusing.

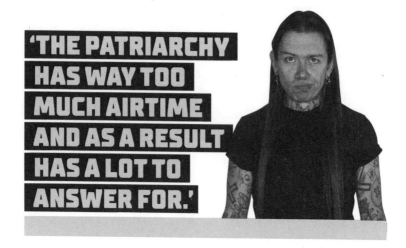

'THE PATRIARCHY HAS WAY TOO MUCH AIRTIME AND AS A RESULT HAS A LOT TO ANSWER FOR.'

The nonsense that fucks me off the most is this tired narrative:

> If you ever want anyone to respect you as a man, then you have to be ripped, super rich, emotionless, provide for everyone, don't let women do anything for themselves because you think they're too weak, be tough, shut up and get on with it – and tell everyone else to do the same.

Projecting that cooked shit into people's heads just fucken scrambles them. What a list of trash to live your life by, right? I can't begin to imagine how a young person who's struggling with their gender identity must feel about being fed all this heavy expectation to 'GENDER UP!' What a useless bummer of a role model the tough guy is for any person. It sucks when you're trying to navigate a super intense world with all of the fucken bananas stuff going on while being told that embodying a bulldozer of a person is the only way you'll survive it. No fucken good!

Now that I've had a moment to get a little older I can see just how fried this traditional idea of what makes a 'real' man is. I really try to make a constant effort to undo the shit in my head and in my behaviour. Sometimes I give myself a pretty fucken hard time about it, but I think it's most certainly worth it to create a more inclusive and less boofhead vibe. Where I can, I try to reflect on my blokey behaviour and any language I may have used, do a bit of checking in with my partner and mates and consider how my conduct could have made people of other genders feel, and even other blokes. For example, a classic worn out performance I try to dodge is shit like opening doors for women but not men. I mean, it's entry-level polite to hold the door open for someone but if you're only doing it for one gender then it's rather odd, don't ya reckon? It's that old-hat stuff men are told that's apparently 'nice' when it's kinda perpetuating weird, old-fashioned behaviour that in reality isn't *that* nice. Rather, it shows you only do things for women for the social congratulations, not because you're nice. Plus this whole men opening doors for women thing comes from some pretty shitty old views that women are 'too weak' to open doors for themselves, which is fucken cooked. Same goes for 'Gday, sweetheart', as calling someone you don't know 'sweetheart' is more creepy than considerate. It can take a sec to check it and go, *Oh yeah, if someone called me that I might feel a little weird.*

It's important for us blokes to listen. Correcting moments where actions need to change is worthwhile because it says you give a shit about other people. I am lucky to have some incredible and patient women in my life who have inspired me to do better; I love them heaps and want to be a better fella for them – and I can't fucken do that if I'm too busy swanning about never being wrong. Being wrong is super powerful stuff, and if you're open to fucking up and making change I think it's pretty rewarding even if it's a little scary from time to time. I still fuck up a bunch but I try to call myself out and change that shit up. (PS I checked in with Jules about this paragraph just to make sure I didn't assume I was right again!)

The concept of becoming a brick wall of a male who's unable to be gentle and kind and take in other views of the world is really heartbreaking to me. It's exhausting having to push away the messages that keep telling you to act like a dickhead; they're everywhere you look, from the advert for the car you want to the guy at work who keeps talking about the fights he gets in, to leaders of entire nations behaving like drunken bros . . . there's seemingly no escape at times. The patriarchy has way too much airtime and as a result has a lot to answer for.

'Boys will be boys' is just an excuse for blokes to act like gronks most of the time. Boys can also not be boys if they choose, and I respect that choice – in fact I love it.

It's suffocating being told what you're supposed to be and how to identify. I can't imagine the harrowing shit that people of other genders have been put through. I know myself and a lot of other men out there have contributed to perpetuating this gronky 'Man Up' nonsense without even noticing. I hope for a future of 'Manning Up' that could employ some broader inclusivity about gender identity and fewer demands about acceptable ways to be.

After having a massive go at us blokes, I think it's also important for me to say that it's fine to be a masculine man and it's okay to feel tough and feel strong and all that stuff, as long as it's not taking everyone's fucken hand bones and social space with it.

How rad would it be if we let other styles of what a man can be thrive and diversify a bit, eh? How about 'Man Up' being redefined as becoming a beautiful rainbow-feathered peacock that also barbecues and cries sometimes while barbecuing? They could be tender and talk about their feelings and wear a bit of makeup from time to time, help others apply theirs but not tell them how to do it, nor be the best at it – and that's okay too. Then 'Man Up' would become such a well-balanced term, it's very possible that it would never need to be said again, 'cause we'd all just be fucken legends instead.

NO PAIN, NO GAIN

The number of bones I have broken is testament to the fact that this cliché is absolute trash – how does breaking your scaphoid in half set you up for any kind of gain? I 'gained' some time without the ability to use my hand properly for quite a while and a prescription for a few painkillers, but that's about it.

What was I set to gain from falling over while trying to kick a ball in wet weather, landing on my arm and snapping the bone so badly it was pointing the wrong direction? A panic attack, that's for sure.

This saying is so super threatening, don't ya think? It brings to mind a tired old gronk saying this shit to people, trying to get them military-level ready for everyday life. Like that bootcamp training shit, where you wake up unnecessarily early in the morning to go get yelled at in an effort to punish yourself for not exercising enough, but all that really happens is you end up hating yourself more because you stopped going, because let's be honest, it was shit. But you *still* give yourself a hard time because you didn't go through

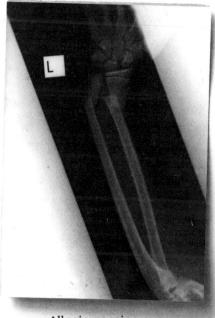

All pain, no gain.

enough 'pain' to 'gain' to look like that airbrushed and photoshopped unit in the fitness magazine.

This 'no pain, no gain' attitude is super overwhelming to digest. It can be applied to so many situations and become the very thing that also ruins them. It's a mindset that is thrown around in the fitness universe constantly, yet if you are experiencing pain you're probably doing it wrong or about to slip a fucken disc instead of piling on the gains, ya lord. I'm on board with the idea that you need to put in a bit of effort occasionally, it's kind of basic science that moving your body around is in general a good thing, and I get that you need to use effort to do it – but to what point?

I remember buying this hectic-looking bamboo pillow from a kiosk at the mall once, thinking *Oh this looks all very precious and ergonomic and bamboo and wow*. Fucken took it home and slept on it, all very excited to become a brand-new man with an amazing well-rested outlook on life. Unfortunately that plan didn't go as planned. Instead I woke up, quite late, reached for something on my bedside table and

threw my neck out so fucken badly that I had to call for help. Jules and my bestie Matty each had to rush from their separate workplaces and come gingerly get me out of bed and take me to the doctor. But 'no pain, no gain', right?

Didn't end there. I went to a local GP (not my usual doctor), walked into the office all twisted up, eyes watering in agony, and maybe I missed the poster in the hallway that said 'No pain, no gain' 'cause this doctor refused to give me proper pain relief, possibly because he thought I still had more to gain from the experience. (More likely it had something to do with the number of tattoos I have, which unfortunately can be a hindrance, shall we say, at any new doctor's office I go to.) So I fucken left with some piss-poor anti-inflam that did nothing, went home and consequently yelled every time I moved my neck at all for the next two days – I was on the gains hard, clearly. Whenever I got into bed, I gained really hard and yelled all about these gains. For the next two days I could barely move for sweet gains, or really do anything except gain my neck off, so I went back to the doc and begged him for some less gains-filled pain relief, and he finally gave me five valium. And while valium was great for the panic attacks caused by receiving such rapid-fire gains, it was of zero fucken help for the pain part. So the gains continued. Jeez was I riding the gains train pretty solidly by this point.

Another two days went by and Jules and I felt as a team that I had gained all I could from the pain, so decided – not entirely sure why – to go back to the same doctor YET

AGAIN, though this time I took Jules in with me to prove I wasn't some kind of drug-hungry beast and was in fact just a fella in a shitload of pain. After a solid questionnaire about my lifestyle habits, he decided to end the training session and give me actual fucking pain relief. It seemed the gains train had pulled up at its last stop, as almost immediately after taking the first dose of the new medicine, my neck was free from any more excruciating gaining.

Let me tell you what I 'gained' from that:

FUCK ALL!

If anything, I gained new respect for how much a shit pillow can fuck you up, the insight to not return to that medical practice, and the lesson that I should probably take Jules with me to any new doctors' appointments from now on.

This 'no pain, no gain' mentality is more or less suggesting you need to fuck yourself up or you're not doing it properly, eh? There's so much of this ridiculous alpha nonsense out there that says 'Have zero fun, get on with it', and it all sucks massive shit and can get on its bike as far as I'm concerned. You'll sooner fucken have a burnout trying to follow the advice of all these cringey motivational posters than see so-called results in whatever you're endeavouring to achieve.

This all-or-nothing energy is what will break your fucken head before you gain anything worth having. You hear stories about these mega-rich units spending every spare second of their life at work because ya 'gotta grind, boi' to make that cash. This constant message of needing to capitalise on everything is what's making it near impossible to afford food and rent for a lot of people. You don't need to have all the things or make a zillion fucken dollars to have a happy, worthwhile life. In fact, a lot of rich people are super unhappy. Sometimes pretty good is pretty good enough. A powerful devotion to cash is likely gonna leave a person super unhappy or with few meaningful relationships when nothing is more important than their desire to make more money, but to what end? So they can die young covered in heaps of it? And hey, sometimes doing things for other people that don't make you money and instead just make someone else's life a little easier is pretty rad too.

Clichéd sayings like this shit me to tears, as do motivational waffle-ons preaching clapped-out advice. Can someone tell me why they always feature either ripped people standing in front of sunsets, or pictures of unclimbable mountains? Yeah I get it, I can't climb that or look that good right now, so what? 'EXPERIENCE PAIN UNTIL YOU DO!'

'SOMETIMES PRETTY GOOD IS PRETTY GOOD ENOUGH.'

These are some of my favourite encourage-you-to-burn-out expressions to hate on:

'YOU GOTTA BE IN IT TO WIN IT'

No you don't. The whole racket of online entrepreneurs trying to make people feel like their lives are just shit 'cause they aren't drop-kicking all their disposable income into property is pretty entitled and irritating.

'THE PAIN WILL LEAVE ONCE IT HAS FINISHED TEACHING YOU'

Can you seriously calm the masochistic fuck down? What kind of self-loathing shit is this? It screams of low self-esteem peddling shit where you feel you deserve to go through torment because of some magical demon that told you you're not worthy of any joy in your life. This one makes me puke in my mouth and is hugely probbo for so many reasons.

'EVERYTHING YOU WANTED TO BE IS ON THE OTHER SIDE OF FEAR'

Scare the shit out of yourself or you won't be happy.

'LIFE IS A DARING ADVENTURE OR NOTHING AT ALL'

Really? Is there no chill in your life at all? Does every moment of your life have to be so riveting that The Rock himself would barely be able to handle the action? Sometimes a pizza on the couch and staying up till 4 am finishing the whole season of a show is cool too, just saying.

'ALL OR NOTHING'

More or less the same level of trite as the 'no pain, no gain' thing, it's clearly not physically possible to go at any average speed in life for whoever's championing this one. They have to give absolutely everything they have to the point of breaking otherwise it's nothing at all, hey? What a fucken shit way to live. The way I see it, you can very easily blow a fucken valve going too hard at an all-or-nothing vibe – you may just go so hard that you deflate the very metaphorical football you were trying to kick between the posts.

'NOTHING WORKS UNLESS YOU DO'

Well not really; heaps of stuff works, and hey – what if you might not be able to work at the moment for reasons like grief, mental health or injury? YOUR FAULT, LOSER!

'EXCUSES DON'T BURN CALORIES'

I have a feeling that the person who came up with this one a) is in great shape, b) doesn't like you being out of shape, c) is rude and d) has very little grasp of what calories are. Calories are a unit of energy measurement and this saying is intended to make you feel so shit about your body and for not exercising that you hate your life.

All of this power-phrase trash riles me up because it's broad-sweeping shit that takes only its own self-congratulations on board and tells everyone else that they are a loser for not thinking the same or getting amongst it. I reckon it's fucked!

I have a few of my own motivational quotes I'd like to rebut with, thanks very much:

'DO WHATEVER THE FUCK YOU WANT AS LONG AS YOU'RE BEING KIND'

Seems accessible and has something for everyone.

'SOME UP-THEMSELVES DOUCHEBAG WROTE THIS SIGN, DON'T WORRY'

Yeah, it was me.

'SUNSETS, MOUNTAINS AND MUSCLES AREN'T THE ONLY THINGS GOING ON IN LIFE'

I feel like it's not a real motivational poster unless it's suggesting heavy amounts of hiking or six-pack challenges with dynamic lighting set-ups.

'NO BRAIN, NO PAIN'

If ya don't have one then ya don't have anything to worry about!

'NO FRET, NO SWEAT'

If you're not fretting about it, you're likely not even sweating about it.

'PUSH YOURSELF TO BREAKING POINT, HAVE A MELTDOWN, RUIN EVERYTHING 'CAUSE YOU WENT TOO HARD'

As it sounds, really: do all that and you'll end up a disastrous mess.

'PARTY ON, JOHN'

My best friend Austin came up with this one. Although it only mentions John's name, it includes everyone in its rhyming slang and of course everyone is invited to party on with John.

'CAN'T TALK, READING SHIT SIGN'

Gotcha!

Kindly chill out and listen to people around you a little more before barking unrequested motivational shit at them. Very rarely has a saying like any of these ever got me off my arse to go be better or do more – it's gone straight to the bin in my head every time. Sure, it's nice when one resonates with you or if it's generally positive, but personally I find being bossed around by sunsets and ripped people saying heavy shit at me nothing but exhausting and irritating.

I LOVE MY OWN FARTS

BE INSPIRED BY THIS STUPID POSTER

With this said, there is nothing wrong with working hard at your goals, which is rad if you have the space to do that shit. Filling your fucken office walls and desktop wallpapers with sayings like 'No pain, no gain' and 'Get rich or die trying', on the other hand, is unnecessary pressure on you to strive for goals you might not be up for. Shit takes time and there is no reason to constantly be in a state of suffering just to move forward in life. Not everything successful in life requires you to go pedal to the metal; you can enjoy a break without it meaning you're nosediving away from your life goals.

I encourage the defacement or sticker-bombing of all motivational signs and posters across the world with the words 'Chill out, sign'. Maybe I'll make some stickers? Probably get in trouble for it, but who gives a shit.

As they say, no pain, no gain, right?

SLEEP
MORE

Thanks for the hot tip there, Einstein. How about you fucken calm down with your sweeping one-size-fits-all magnesium advice, eh?

The pressure of being told to 'sleep more' when you mention how shattered you are is about as unhelpful as not being able to sleep in the first place. As someone who suffers from a chronic sleep disorder, let me tell you that being advised to 'JUST DO IT!' doesn't fucken cut the mustard, champ.

If there's a technique or supplement out there that's supposed to help you sleep, I've bloody tried it and met all its deadshit mates. From the smash hits chamomile tea all the way to sleeping tablets, I've given the lot a run.

Sleeping is a delicate, mysterious part of the universe and one of the great undiscovered wonders of the world for some. If you aren't one of those people who's had trouble sleeping, you are truly very lucky in a way my envious mind can't begin to describe. Without sleep your whole universe gets kicked straight in the guts and all normal day-to-day

function is sent express post to the shit part of town where nothing is open and everyone is sad and can't be fucked.

For argument's sake, let's say you aren't someone who struggles to sleep. You are, of course, still familiar with the sensation of feeling 'tired' or 'sleepy', but now imagine that you're trying to focus on completing a task but all you can think about is not having slept and worrying you'll never sleep again. The preoccupation of wanting to give the dog the bone that is ACTUALLY FUCKEN SLEEP NOW, PLEASE can be as debilitating as the lack of sleep itself. Not being able to sleep yet feeling like you need to is the fucken essence of frustrating brutality, as it messes up all the plans you have in life. The worst part of this dance routine is feeling super wrecked and lying down 'cause you think you'll be able to catch a few z's only to have your mind or body act like an excited puppy. Like having a glass of water snatched away in the desert, it's a moment of desperation where all you want is one thing, but you can't have the thing because 'body says no'.

JULES' TAKE ON SLEEPING MORE

One night when Nat and I were in LA, we were shaken awake by an earthquake. It was a decent one: pictures fell off the walls and it went on for long enough that I had time to mentally race through old American movie references in an attempt to remember what to do. Is it stand in a doorway? Hide under the bed? Will we have time to make it outside? Is outside even worse?

But the main thing that sticks with me from that moment was the split seconds between waking up and panic-deciding a course of action, where I was actually experiencing the whole house shaking, but thought it was Nat having a sleep attack.

His restless leg syndrome means sometimes he's so uncomfortable that all he can do to relieve the pain is shake his limb – sometimes an arm, sometimes a shoulder, sometimes a leg, sometimes all of them at once. I'm often vibrated awake and go into massage mode in an attempt to quieten the incessant ache. In LA, it was only when I glanced over at Nat and saw him dozing peacefully next to me that I realised what was going on.

To anyone who has this condition (or any other sleep-affecting disorder), I'm sorry it sucks so badly. The cruelty of something messing so severely with the sleep that you are so desperate for is intense.

It's okay to feel overwhelmed, you have an earthquake going on inside you. <3

Not being able to sleep is truly infuriating shit at its highest level . . . and then having some fuckwit who *can* sleep telling you all you need is to brew some special tea or rub some stupid fucken oil on your chest and count sheep is about where I start to crack.

Mind you, I've also had the opposite problem before when I had chronic fatigue, and all I could do *was* sleep, though it wasn't exactly the pleasant restorative vibe that I was chasing. I was experiencing chronic fatigue as a result of having tuberculosis, which takes all the fun out of a refreshing kip, let me tell ya. The sleep I was getting was down to the fact I had zero energy because my body was fucken wasting. I would sweat through my clothes when I did manage to sleep, which was fucken annoying 'cause I would wake up covered in sweat and have to change out of my sopping wet rags, which I could absolutely not be fucked doing because I was so . . . wait for it . . . TIRED. Then I'd have to lay towels down on my bed only to sweat through the lot all over again. I did this on repeat for more than six months, practically unconscious most of the day. It was a super fucken shit time.

Sleep has always been a tricky one for me. It has been something I've always wanted to be able to be friends with, but I've never really known how to connect with it. I'm not exactly set up for a win in the sleep department, since I have such an anxious mind – I'm already locked and loaded for a massive lack of sleep victories.

I can't imagine what it's like having a baby and trying to fucken sleep. The sleep deprivation that parents go through is the stuff of nightmares – they use it as a torture tactic for a reason. Having to care for a little person who has zero ability to communicate how they're feeling and just cries like the world is ending must be distressing and maddening, particularly if you're a single parent. Huge respect to parents out there who struggle with that shit. Holy fuck you're a trooper, each and every one of ya.

One of the big things I've noticed about sleep is that having a settled energy is a good start. Trying to quieten the mind is fucken tough work if you're the worrying type, and I am most certainly that type. The end of the day, after all the regular life stuff has stopped, is when the anxious mind goes mining for golden fuck-you moments. It sets up a slide night for you to watch – whether you want to or not – that's full of distressing shit you really don't need to be looking at while trying to catch a break. 'Oh remember that dumb shit you said or did ten years ago?' BAM! 'Now try to fall asleep, dickhead.'

Of course you can't because the evil mind DJ won't stop beat-matching shit memories, so what do you do? You reach for your phone to distract yourself and just bulldoze a bunch more stupid trash into your head, over-stimulating yourself further in more unhelpful ways, only to see even poorer results.

What the fuck are you supposed to do in these dense tired moments? As with all things you put in your body, I'd probably speak to a health professional before you freestyle yourself into the hospital or worse, but for me there have been a few supposedly big-ticket items that just don't deliver. Let me run you through a dozen of the massive sleep fails I've made over the years.

1. MAGNESIUM SUPPLEMENTS/ RUBBING OILS

If this works for you, then fuck yeah, party on, Wayne. I don't wanna pooh-pooh your victory with magnesium if it has managed to help you, but personally if I have to hear this hot tip again I'm going to implode like a star. Now, while I understand that magnesium is essential for your body, it's also not necessarily the holy grail of sleep aids some claim it to be. It's been suggested to me as a solution more times than I've had hot dinners in my entire life and it's getting so old it likely owns an autographed bible. In fact, it's now a joke between me and my mates who also have trouble sleeping; we DM each other 'have you tried magnesium, tho?' and the laugh we get from it is probably more help than magnesium ever was.

I have tried hundreds of variations of magnesium powders, rubbing oils, sprays and tablets, self-medicating like I'm some kind of new-age wizard, to no avail. With that said, I have enjoyed some more calming moments after taking it, but that was likely a placebo effect from thinking the $80 powder I'd bought with 'super-duper sleep magnesium' on the label is gonna be a shoo-in.

2. MELATONIN TABLETS

How about a sleep hormone your body naturally produces that comes in tablet form for if you don't feel your body is serving you enough? It's not supposed to be used as a long-term solution and can give you super vivid dreams, which is fucken annoying, but luckily for me I have an adverse reaction to it anyway whereby it sets off my restless leg syndrome (RLS), so I can't be dabbling in this shit. I've heard you can kick off a release of your body's own melatonin by drinking a warm glass of milk before bed, which is great if you're not lactose intolerant. Sadly, extra melatonin hasn't done a great deal of anything for me and rather has given my restlessness permission to shine.

3. PROMETHAZINE

For some RLS sufferers, this medication can strap a fucken supercharger to it and drive you straight to hell. It can bring on a fun dose of deathly tiredness while also making your joints ache in a desperation to move them, or else the sensation of them exploding in agony. I steer well clear of this one.

4. SLEEP SHRED SUPPLEMENTS

Talk about shiny packaging selling you an apparently magical two-in-one product! These 'street legal' supps are full of more shit than a used car salesman. Don't get me started on how expensive this weight loss sleep shred crap is, and how they're more likely to send your heart racing out the door than put you in a state of peaceful rest. The 'shred' part of these products usually implies that they are not only going to knock you out but also help you lose fat at the same time.

As my old man says, 'If it sounds too good to be true, it probably is.' These fucken powders skate a very thin line between giving you panic attack levels of restlessness and being useless garbage; often they have melatonin in them to help counteract the elevated heart rate caused by some of the other ingredients, so they claim to help you sleep, but as I mentioned before, I react badly to melatonin so I've already shot myself in the jangling foot there. And anyway, you'd be forgiven for missing it among the 700 other ingredients in these things.

I'm sure it works for some, but rolling the dice by ingesting a supplement with more random chemicals in it than a meth lab doesn't sit right with me as a sleep solution.

5. ELECTRIC FAN

I love a good fan session, particularly during the Sydney summer (which gets fucken hot). At one stage I was such a 'fan' of the 'fan' that I had two of the fucken things facing me at once at full pelt – it felt like sleeping inside a small cyclone. Nonetheless, I grew so accustomed to this routine and the sound of the fans that I'd carry it into the winter months. I thought I could be tricky and still have the fans on in the cold if I just pointed them away from me. Nope. Eventually, the cold air would recirculate around the room and freeze the fuck out of me, henceforth freezing me back awake.

6. HERBAL TEA

Well for a start, let me tell you that while green tea seems like a very calming option, it contains caffeine, so I don't recommend that move. There's a sea of herbal teas out there with the word *sleep* written on them, coupled with images of starry nights and other waffle designed to trick you into thinking it will make you sleepy. In the end they usually do absolute fuck-all. I should point out that smashing a bunch of hectic calming teas before bed will sooner have you back up for a piss than it will get you to a state of blissful rest. In general, I am not the kind of person to do things by halves, so it's often two bags at once when it comes to brewing a cuppa. In terms of flavour, it's not always the biggest bang for your buck, the old herbal tea, which is why

I bung two bags in the one cup – it probably says a lot about me as a person, really. So any piss-in-the-wind benefits the chamomile, lavender and peppermint crowd were supposed to have are well outweighed by the need to use the bathroom in the hours following.

7. ALCOHOL

Do I really have to explain why this is a shit idea? Probably not, but I will anyway! From a scientific perspective, it's a lose-lose situation. Though booze can help you get to sleep due to its sedative properties, eventually it turns on ya and becomes a stimulant that leads to more disrupted, poorer-quality sleep during the second half of the night – or wakes you back up completely and sends you for a piss faster than you can say hangover. Chuck on top that you feel like microwaved catshit the next day and I think we can all agree that getting on the beers is a terrible solution for sleep.

8. BAR OF SOAP UNDER THE SHEETS

Yes, you heard that right. I read somewhere that putting a bar of soap under your bedsheets is supposed to help relieve restlessness. It fascinates me how this has worked for anyone. Yet it still seemed like a pretty safe thing for me to try, and sure enough, it did . . . fuck all!

'TRYING TO QUIETEN THE MIND IS FUCKEN TOUGH.'

9. SLEEPING PILLS

The 'ripping the hand brake' option here. Obviously, there's a bunch of sleeping pills that do work, but they aren't the safest shit on Earth, certainly not in the long term. What's more, feeling like a fucken ghoul the following day isn't exactly the desired result I'm after when I wake up from eight hours of shut-eye.

10. WATCHING TV

Falling asleep in front of the telly is a true classic, seems harmless and kinda nice sometimes . . . but the key word there is 'sometimes'. Historically, I could very rarely get to sleep without having some kind of sitcom TV on, usually because I was fighting off a panic attack at bedtime. For a few years, a sitcom with maniacal laughing going on in the background was the only thing that made me feel like I wasn't going to die of panic at night. The problem with this technique as a solution is that while it helped me get to sleep, it also stopped me from resting properly, as the blue light from the screen along with the constant noise of canned laughter is more stimulating than relaxing.

Remember that if you are sharing a bed with someone else, they tend to get the shits with it too, particularly if they don't have issues falling asleep. Well, with late-night comedy re-runs blaring at them, they do now!

It's also important to point out that your choice of show makes a big difference, as you have to find the sweet spot between funny and not too interesting or engaging, otherwise you'll stay up and watch it properly, and then the next episode. I have gone hard with the uninteresting side of sitcoms and successfully bored myself to sleep thanks to a DVD of the god-awful *Two and a Half Men*, only to wake up to the theme song of 'manly men men men, mennnnnn' being played on repeat, which – let me tell you – ruins everything. Choose your comedy viewing wisely, champions!

The TV distraction might be great as a bandaid solution but it has to turn off at some stage or you just end up waking to laughter, which is sometimes pleasant, though sometimes it feels like you're being laughed at for sleeping like an arsehole.

11. COUNTING SHEEP

You can rely on this flogged load of inaccessible advice to piss you off more than it does help you rest. If I wanted to do some monotonous trash to get myself to sleep, I would sooner listen to an audio book of how to assemble IKEA furniture before I would repetitively count the same farm animal. What shit advice this is.

12. MEDITATION

Meditating is sterling shit if you can manage it, but it can
backfire if you put too much stress on yourself to be good
at it too fast. I find it exceptionally difficult because it means
I'm not allowed to distract myself from the bullshit in my
head. Trying to sit still and actively avoid thinking about all
the stuff my brain is super keen to entertain me with is like
placing a raw steak in front of a dog and telling it to 'stay'.
It may sit still for a second or two, but as soon as you look
away . . . BANG! It's feeding time. Meditation is a bit of a long-
game kinda thing from what I understand. Rome wasn't built
in a day and all that. Well worth a shot for general calm in
one's life, but not exactly a quick fix for the anxious sleeper.

The list goes on and on and on, from white noise machines to
acupressure mats to compression massage, I've tried it all.

Sadly, the chances are it doesn't work for me.

**'SLEEPING IS A DELICATE,
MYSTERIOUS PART
OF THE UNIVERSE AND
ONE OF THE GREAT
UNDISCOVERED WONDERS
OF THE WORLD FOR SOME.'**

There are some things I have found beneficial and wholesome, though.

SHIT THAT HAS ACTUALLY HELPED

Running: Running is hard any way you look at it, but during lockdown I wasn't able to go to the gym so I started doing this satanic shit. I kinda fucken hate it, but I can't argue that it hasn't changed the game for rest. The days I go on runs, I sleep way better, damnit!

Therapy: 'Cause talking about shit out loud saves you having to repeat it at yourself while you try to fall sleep.

Eating enough during the day: Nothing like a solid caloric deficit to make sleep near impossible. Finding out that you need actual energy to sleep baffled me at first but now makes sense.

Feeling happy: A rare occasion for me, but when I have gone to bed happy I have slept so much better.

Sleeping somewhere else: Preferably near the ocean, but even the couch or at a mate's place will do in a pinch. The beach one has worked so many fucken times. Whether it's the calming sound of waves or the fact I have tricked my brain with some new scenery, say what you want, it's actually helped.

There are loads of unhealthy ones I'll leave out, but you get the idea. In the end not one of them is a sure thing, really. The mind wins every time.

Everyone is different, sleep is unique to each of us, and for some it's a very precious and elusive thing. It's super beneficial in loads of different ways, not only for your physical health but to help your mind take a much-needed break from the world. Not being able to sleep can be an all-consuming problem – people fascinate over it, I know I do. That fascination can end up in really dangerous places for some, and I really feel for those people, so working out what's causing it is a worthwhile goal. The journey to better sleep can be a tough one, and it's often a head game rather than a powdered one.

So next time some well-slept hero who's feeling oh so proud of themselves comes at you with their magnesium chats and calming tea prattle, tell 'em ya can't talk right now and go for a run – away from them and their trash advice. You'll work it out one day, sooner by your own navigation of your mind than double dumping mushroom powders and flower tablets up your guts.

Phwoooar, fuck mate, don't get me started on this fucken health halo bullshit. I have spent waaay too much of my spare time for the better part of the past five years reading and listening to research on so-called 'healthy living'. There has been no shortage of late-night viewing of cherry-picking, info-ed up fitness fuckwits on YouTube talking about types of food and exercise and whether certain versions of both are either 'good' or 'bad' for you. I have embraced it pretty obsessively at times, to the point where, if you know me personally, you might say I have become quite the pain in the arse about it all. Over the last few years I have lost more than 30 kg (66 lb) of weight, though by no stretch does this mean I have any right to be dishing out advice on the topics of weight loss, meal plans, bootcamps or yoga poses. I am one of many of the self-researched lords who think they know better, and the irony I suppose is that it's worked for me, so I feel especially entitled to my opinion.

While some of this wellness journey has been positive, I have consequently taken a lot of the blissful ignorance and fun out of food for myself in the process, having counted every single fucking calorie and nutrient going into my body like some kind of terminator in an effort to lose excess weight and get healthier. I don't look at food the same way now; I scan it – I've had a calorie-counter surgically implanted in my brain, and it sucks 'cause I can't turn the fucken thing off. It makes going out for a random meal at a restaurant become a stress-filled analysis session where I imagine the chef using wild amounts of oil and butter while sparks start flying out of my fucking ears in distress. It doesn't sit well with the inner control freak.

'I'VE HAD A FEW HAIRY ADVENTURES WITH OBSESSING OVER FOOD AND VITAMIN INTAKE AND IT BACKFIRING ON ME.'

Regardless of all my flexing here, this obsession *has* also gifted me a massive bullshit detector for rubbish health advice. I have tried plenty of stupid diets and restrictive eating patterns in my time; a lot of them were fucken cooked and a fair few messed with my head. I eventually sought some professional assistance to help improve my lifestyle, which has been a power move, but champion, you better believe it hasn't stopped me from cracking the mega shits at 'health food advice' on the reg.

For example, when I hear 'an apple a day keeps the doctor away' my head explodes with rage-filled numbers. I think it's broad sweeping nonsense such as this nursery-rhyme-level cliché that bamboozles the everyday person with unexplained health advice garbage, since some might

LIFE: WHAT NAT TO DO

take it to mean: 'Okay, so an apple a day keeps the doctor away, does it? So I just eat an apple every day then I don't need to see a doctor or change the rest of the horrendous lifestyle choices I make?' No it does not – that's not how apples work, mate. In fact they're only one of *maaany* things that make up a potentially healthy diet, not a diet otherwise made up entirely of craft beer and frozen dim sims.

See, I'm already fucken doing it! Didn't take fucken long, eh? I'm already part of the problem, dishing out this advice myself . . . take it with a grain of salt, champion, but oh god, wait – salt comes with its own blood pressure raising issues. There is no escape. But seriously, talk to a qualified medical professional would ya – this is intended as a work of comedy, not a health guide.

Until then my ramble will continue, so suffer in ya jocks.

The expression 'an apple a day keeps the doctor away' is a stupid one dating from 1913 and was adapted from some other old nineteenth-century proverb that said:

**Eat an apple on going to bed, and you'll keep
the doctor from earning his bread.**

So listen here, turbo with the willy-nilly apple advice. Apples are a fucken terrible choice of food to eat before bed, ya big dickhead. This is why:

On average an apple has about 4.5 g of fibre and 13 g of sugar in each one – yes, it is natural sugar, but nonetheless, coupled with the high fibre content it's quite an efficient, slow-burning energy source and not one you should consume before bed unless you're chasing an evening of thrashing around pretending to sleep. Last time I checked, sleep deprivation wasn't a lifestyle change recommendation on high rotation in modern medicine.

My other point is that, aside from what an obviously bad choice it is to smash an apple before bed, it isn't some kind of fucken Harry Potter wand that waves away the need to ever see a doctor again, or never eat any other fresh fruit or veg. I suspect part of the apple-eating argument is that the fibre content of said apple is beneficial to your overall health. While that is true, it's fucken far from the recommended daily intake, which is on average 25–30 g of fibre for an adult. That means to reach the fibre goal you'd need to consume five or six apples a day at 95 calories a ride, which is about 500 calories and enough sugars to jump start a car. I can't see that working out well as a dietary move, and though I'm sure there are plenty of worse ideas out there, it isn't exactly an untouchable healthcare plan.

I've had a few hairy adventures with obsessing over food and vitamin intake and it backfiring on me, so let me share a few with ya here.

A couple of years ago I wanted to lean out a bit before I went on my stand-up tour, I suppose so I would

feel a little less self-conscious when in front of thousands of
people. But I didn't want to give up the beers entirely,
so I started researching ways to get more bang for my buck
in the calorie department, opting to eat leaner meat to help
that. I had a protein goal I wanted to hit, so I started eating
tuna, fucken lots of it, several times a day. At this time I had
zero idea that it contained a high level of a substance called
purines. Now, purines are chemical compounds that are
broken down into uric acid when metabolised, but if your
body can't metabolise purines effectively, this can result
in elevated levels of uric acid, which can increase the
chances of suffering from kidney stones, gout and other
shit stuff. Most people do not need to worry themselves
about purine content in foods because they break it down
into uric acid that is then dissolved in the blood, passed
through the kidneys into urine and eliminated from the
body no problemo . . . I, on the other hand, have a hereditary
predisposition to getting gout, which I had been informed of

by my relatives a bunch of times whenever they'd say to me things along the lines of: 'You're gonna get it one day, mate.' For some reason I seemed to think that was bullshit and kept on keeping on with the tsunami of tuna sashimi.

'LAST TIME I CHECKED, SLEEP DEPRIVATION WASN'T A LIFESTYLE CHANGE RECOMMENDATION ON HIGH ROTATION IN MODERN MEDICINE.'

Of course, I had no idea that an excess of certain lifestyle factors can bring on an attack of gout, and I had made my own brand-new freestyle dietary decision to eat a stupid amount of tuna every day along with the occasional way-too-many beers. It was a combination that didn't make a heap of sense in terms of slimming down, but I thought one kinda made way for the other, not realising that, in fact, even worse than tuna in the purine department was the brewer's yeast used to make, that's right: beer! So not only was I eating like a fuckwit and still drinking what was probably stopping me from losing the couple of extra kilograms, I was also on an express train to Gout City.

I had started to take massive walks to help along the weight loss, as every self-appointed health and fitness expert likes to toss in some physical activity with their questionable dietary choices, and it was working okay. Slowly the kilos went down, but my foot – Jesus, my foot started to hurt.

By this point my tour was underway and I was of course doing stand-up, so a lot of standing up was involved. The more I did it the more the foot hurt, and eventually my foot was so fucken swollen I had to remove the insole from my shoe, and then before long I couldn't even fit it in the fucken thing.

I was hoping desperately that this wasn't gout. All I could hear in my head was a relative's voice on repeat: 'You're gonna get it one day, mate.' Fuck, really? Surely it was all the walking that was causing my foot to swell up?

Eventually I was in so much agony I could barely take a few steps, I was yelling like a stuck pig in the hotel every night, crying out in pain, begging the universe to make it stop. The pain was something I had never experienced in my fucken life. The only way to describe it is it felt like someone smashed my foot with the back end of a cricket bat. It FUCKING HURT! Like, so much. There's something to be said about an extremity in such agonising pain that it can't be alleviated, it just takes your breath away. So, as much as it scares the fuck out of me, I had to go to a doctor. Thankfully one of Jules' relatives is a doctor and could see me late at night at his house, the legend, as we drove through Queensland to the next town I'd be performing at.

He had a quick look at it, pressed the big red bit on the edge of my toe and said something to the tune of 'Yeah, looks like gout.'

Fuuuuck nooo, don't let my family be right! To be certain, the doc sent me for blood work and sure as shit it came back like a fucken person with two Maglites on an airstrip waving you down yelling 'GOUT!' I was then prescribed a medication that you have to take until the pain goes away or you get the runs. I shat myself and the pain didn't go away, for four months. There was only meant to be a week or two of suffering but it went on for four . . . fucking . . . months. I even had to buy a pair of shoes one size bigger, for fuck's sake.

I looked up what may have brought on the gout and sure enough, tuna and beer were at the top of the list.

Fuck, I felt like an idiot. I did the rest of the tour with it, two shows a night for weeks at a time – totally fucken sucked. It has taken more than a year to recover from and my foot still isn't the same.

The lesson here, friends, is that making dietary or lifestyle changes based on late nights watching YouTube, or without talking to a medical, dietary or other appropriate professional is a fucken poor move.

There's such a tidal wave of annoying health food information out there telling you it's the holy grail of healthy living, it can be overwhelming and confusing. That's why people's relationships with food are often stressful. There're so many products boasting 'wellness' and other irritating health-halo terms like superfood, high protein, low carb etc. that are merely ways to sell you shit and not get you match fit.

MY TOP FIVE SHIT BUZZWORDS TO TRICK YOU INTO THINKING YOU'RE BEING A RADICAL HEALTH LORD

1. Low-carb Beer

This stupid shit totally fucks me off. It may come as a shock to you but beer isn't a health food, soz about it – not even the low-carb kind. The very evil carbohydrates you've tried to avoid aren't really what you should be focusing on at the bottle-o, since both regular and low-carb beer contains the same level of alcohol, which is high in kilojoules. And even though alcohol is technically a macronutrient, it's not essential, and isn't necessary for sustaining life (unlike the three essential macronutrients: protein, fat and – spoiler – *carbohydrates*). My point is, once you've had any alcohol at all you can forget worrying about any of your macros, bucko, as your now poisoned body prioritises the alcohol as fuel, not the carbs, fats or proteins. Low-carb beer is just called that because the words 'carbs' and 'weight loss' are old nonsense to encourage you to buy this stuff when you think it's better for you than normal-levels-of-carbs beer.

2. High Protein/Source of Protein

Yes, this particular high-protein frozen ham and cheese pizza pocket is higher in protein than a regular version, but alongside all that protein is a terrifying amount of saturated fats and other gnarly shit that is not good for you on the regular. High protein's best mate, 'source of protein,' is like saying 'this water has wet stuff in it' or 'this has something in it you've heard you need to have but no idea how much'. Protein is important, but if you have no idea how much you need I wouldn't rely on a bowl of cereal to get you there.

3. Superfood

It wears a cape and flies around fighting crime, does it? Not really; it's just a marketing term used to imply that this food is better than all the other food out there. There's a chance that it's great for you, but so is eating a wide variety of other shit that doesn't claim to be the absolute best. Not all food has to be super-duper all the time to be good for ya.

4. Low Fat

Doesn't that sound nice – low fat must mean I will be less fat if I eat it? Not really. See, the thing is, usually the products with 'low fat' blasted all over them are also good mates with a higher sugar content. Having a label that calls attention to anything's 'High Sugar' content probably won't move product as well as saying it's low fat. Maybe that's why they leave that bit out!

5. High Fibre

Fucken oath, fibre is the best, but if you're trying to get your daily fibre from heavily processed and refined cereal you may also be ticking a few other less healthy boxes while you're at it without realising. Like everything else in the nutrient universe, there is a recommended daily quantity as well as advice on the quality of the source you're getting the nutrient from. Fibre's highest scoring players are the quiet cool ones that don't feel the need to have colourful stickers all over them: fruit and vegetables, nuts, seeds, brown rice and wholegrain flour. As breathtaking as own-brand bran flakes are, I prefer to nail my fibre intake with something that doesn't taste like an old cupboard.

I have learnt from trying heaps of these questionable delicacies that there is no magic diet that makes you a perfectly healthy person. Eating good food and food that makes you happy is more likely to do you good than a packet of frozen pasta dinner branded 'extra healthy dinna' that comes in a green box to trick your brain into thinking it's gonna deliver on those nutrition goals. That's not to say that from time to time, 'bad' food can't be just what your mood is looking for, as ya need a bit of nonsense in your life to keep it interesting, don't you? If you ate like some kind of virtuous robot you'd be miserable and end up hating all food, which is something that genuinely scares me. Food is such wonderful stuff, so remember that you're never gonna get a diet perfectly right all the time, and nor should you.

'THERE'S SUCH A TIDAL WAVE OF ANNOYING HEALTH FOOD INFORMATION OUT THERE.'

Happiness is the diet that works, and if that means a bit of shit food, then bring it the fuck on. I have a propensity for buying cheap and nasty meat pies when I'm on the road.

They aren't exactly a life-affirming choice, more a terrifying hidden mystery UFO full of who-knows-what, but I love them, even if they're kinda shit. I just hammer one with sauce and smile through the maggot-bag glory. Trying to fit whatever the fuck was in it into my calorie counting app is a waste of time, and that's a good thing, as sometimes I need to give it a rest.

What I have learnt is that listening to your body and your arse is more reliable than taking advice from some made-up Dr Dickhead on the internet who turns out to be a chiropractor in the end and not a GP or dietician.

Eat what makes ya happy!

Just don't eat jar sauce. That shit will kill ya ;)

WHAT DOESN'T KILL YOU MAKES YOU STRONGER

! Heads-up champions, if you're living with medical anxiety, then this chapter comes with a warning of potentially distressing content.

113

O nce upon a time about eleven years ago, I was pushing my motorcycle inside my garage only to feel a sudden sharp pain in my left shoulder. I thought, *Gee, this feels a bit fucken shit. Hope I'm not having a fucken heart attack.*

I wasn't in the greatest shape of my life back then so a few question marks were whizzing around my noggin. I had previously been diagnosed with tuberculosis, so knew my lungs weren't the best – I'd even recently started experiencing a hissing sound when I exhaled. I took myself to see a rando GP who told me it was just asthma and was sent packing without anyone even listening to my chest. *Surely a pain in my shoulder can't be my lungs*, I thought to myself. I then noticed my breathing becoming progressively shallower, as if there was some kind of ceiling to it, so I did what any respectable citizen of the medical anxiety community would do and jumped on Google to self-diagnose the issue.

Of all the honorary doctorates on Earth you can give yourself, the medical doctorate is probably not the smartest one to claim with zero training. Not only does becoming a doctor of medicine take a fucken long time to achieve, but it's also a very complex and responsibility-filled area of work to be in. Nonetheless, I was up to the job. I managed to give myself several conflicting diagnoses that poorly bandaided the severe panic attacks I was having on repeat. I was being treated for pretty severe mental health problems during this time and was on a range of hectic medications to help manage them. One of those was an antipsychotic medicine that would absolutely drop me like it was hot, so in my exhausted state of studious genius I decided the best course of action was to just drug myself to sleep so that the shoulder pain would magically go away during my catatonic slumber.

Well would you believe it? It absolutely did quite the opposite and I woke up fucking shitting the gear because my breathing was frighteningly short and shallow. I gave it up and called my actual GP and not a random one up the road. He suggested I head to him quick smart, so I did just that, jumped in a cab and raced to the doctor's surgery and was sent immediately to get an X-ray. The results were so exciting that they decided this was a job for the hospital. Let me fucken tell ya, champion,  Easter long weekend at the hospital was truly a bad choice timing-wise, with emergency fucken chock-a-block full of people who had varying levels of injuries and some poor locals who were struggling with drug addiction issues. I kinda looked like both crowd demos, to be honest.

From there a doctor came to visit me and told me that I had a collapsed lung aka spontaneous pneumothorax (great band name idea, by the way). They were going to perform a procedure where they needed to knock a few holes between my ribs and feed some tubes into said lung to let the nonsense drain out of it WHILE I WAS AWAKE. This all sounded suitably fucking terrifying, particularly given I'm someone with an anxiety disorder, so my head wasn't really feeling like this was a Good Friday.

To help you imagine what was in store for me, ask anyone who has had their ribs tattooed how much that shit hurts. I have had my ribs tattooed before and that needle only went a few millimetres deep; this shit was going the whole fucken way into my *fucken lung*! In terms of levels of shit that sounds fucked, this is up the top of that cooked pyramid of No Thanks. But there was no other option. I couldn't walk this one off, tough guy.

'IT'S SUCH AN IMPORTANT THING TO TALK TO DOCTORS WHEN YOU'RE NOT FEELING WELL.'

Thankfully the hospital offered me some morphine to help calm me the fuck down 'cause I was not happy with the direction my Easter long weekend was taking. I was pretty dosed out, so this may not be word-for-word accurate, but I remember being asked to put my arm above my head and to relax and expect to feel a little bit of pressure. Fucken right I felt some pressure! They cut a hole in the side of my body and bashed some rod thing into my lung! I bloody carried on quite a bit because it was really fucken scary and quite traumatic, but this was my lucky mental health day as I then found out they actually needed to do this procedure twice. Yay!

They fed a couple of tubes in through the holes in my side and attached them to a weird little box that bubbled away with the fluid that was draining from my chest.

I sat there for a while, pretty off it. I was in agony and distress, and the morphine wasn't quite pulling its weight, unfortunately. I think it was heaps worse because of how traumatised I'd been by what had just happened. What's more, I could hear plenty of other patients moaning in pain too, which really added to the tranquility of this day spa.

I know from being tattooed a great deal that if you start to feel emotional distress from the pain and panic about it, it becomes a thousand times worse. I think this was very much the case in this instance. Huge shout-out to the docs, nurses, paramedics and emergency workers out there and all you deal with on a daily basis; the levels of constant distress served to you must be huge. I definitely chipped in to that vibe and truly made such a commotion about the whole event, to the point where I was trying to bargain with the medics to give me more pain relief, which is not a great look when you're covered in tattoos. The gang at the hospital let me know that I had in fact received the maximum amount of morphine permitted for this Easter lunch, but not all was lost, as there was another option available:

Ketamine!

Now to reiterate, I was not exactly 'myself' or writing down a step by step in my diary about this whole moment, but I'm pretty sure I said to the kind person offering me ketamine that I didn't like ketamine and that it spun me out. Don't ask me how I know this, but I do. I certainly don't think this was my finest moment in life, but I was just being honest. My only options at this point were a) sit there in pain punishing the whole triage team like a classroom full of kids at a recorder lesson or b) just neck up and take the horse tranquilliser. I picked the K, er I mean ketamine, and let me tell ya, it was true to form and sent me express post to hell.

I went into what is known to certain partygoers as a DEFCON 1 level K-hole. A sensation I can only describe as a classic hits dissociative panic attack that feels like you're leaving your body with a jet pack strapped to your back. It was severe enough that I wasn't able to talk properly – or at all – which I think was probably a good thing for everyone else, 'cause I was really on one with the running commentary. Strangely, given all the parties I've forgotten the details of, this one I remember way more vividly than I would prefer, thinking people were coming to get me and all sorts of harrowing shit, all while unable to speak. I'm sure I was dribbling some kind of strange moaning noises as well. I can only describe it as feeling trapped in my own body with a couple of brand-new holes punched in one side of it and a PlayStation 1 attached to the other, sucking out my will to live. I then passed out and don't remember the rest, thank god.

I woke up who the fuck knows how much later, but the show was faaaaaar from over, friends. My lung drain was still bubbling away when it should have stopped long ago. This signals that the lung isn't repairing the way it should, woo hoo! Of course, I was loving this news. The medical team then decided to send me for an MRI, which if you didn't already know is like an X-ray machine's tough older sibling. Imagine a whirring, clicking magnetic doughnut anus that you're slid in and out of like you're on some awful, low-octane local fair ride. It's a real time.

It was super nice of them to let me take my lung drain with me (sarcasm: I didn't have a choice) since managing a small box of bubbling lung juice with two hoses connecting it to your busted lung while you're propelled through a hole in a backless paper gown is a real dream come true.

After that barrel of laughs, I was wheeled back out to my bed in the pumping emergency department and shortly afterwards I was visited by a doctor who had just seen the pictures they took of me on the magical magnetic merry-go-round. Awesome news: they had found a tennis ball sized cyst in my lung. I was then informed quite casually that half my lung can get in the bin; that is, they planned to remove a good whack of my lung when they went in to cut out the cyst. It felt like all my anxiety Christmases had come at once and I could finally flourish into the truly validated medically anxious wreck I knew I was inside.

They removed the cooked part of the lung. It sucked.

I woke up in bed with a massive slice down my back that was stapled shut and all sorts of exciting shit hanging off me. I spent some time in intensive care being kept an eye on. One of my cool new additions was an epidural that went directly into my spine. And there I was thinking this stuff was reserved for women in labour! Part of my chest was numb, including bits of it that weren't where the lung incision was. Of all of the wild shit attached to me, the one that shocked me most was the catheter that took me a whole day to discover. It's hard to explain what it's like seeing something coming out of your genitals and having no idea how it got there. It scared the fuck out of me. I wanted it out immediately for some odd reason, and assured the medical team I was able to urinate independently even though I was on a busload of pain killers. I'm sure they discouraged it but eventually they let me have a crack at it.

Massive mistake.

They gave me a time frame in which to do a wee in a jug, otherwise the hose was garn right back in, champ. I was determined to not have that thing fed back up my urethra, so I used all the focus I could to try to wee into the jug while lying down. Fuck, it's so hard – even standing up on that many painkillers is hard, which I was about to learn. The clock was ticking and if I couldn't make it happen then I was in trouble.

'IT'S HARD TO EXPLAIN WHAT IT'S LIKE SEEING SOMETHING COMING OUT OF YOUR GENITALS AND HAVING NO IDEA HOW IT GOT THERE.'

What followed was a rather embarrassing moment for me. Though I was pretty off my face, mildly panicking and hugely distressed, I felt that asking Mum to help me stand so I could wee into a jug while she held a towel up to protect my privacy was the only option I had. Try as I might, the inner stage fright was too powerful. Even thinking of rivers, waterfalls and cases of beer didn't unlock the floodgates: nothing could beat the morphine's effect on my brain–bladder connection; it was as if the whole world was there watching me, rather than just my poor mum.

Time was up, and the rest is unpleasant history.

After I left hospital, the lack of morphine in my life became pretty shit pretty quick. I stayed with Mum for a bit, eventually the painkillers ran out and I didn't know I could get another dose to help manage the agony. I remember writhing and crying desperately in pain for many nights with my amazing partner staying by my side consoling me while I was lost, not knowing what to do with all the pain. As the painkillers wore off I had a huge withdrawal and got a really heavy case of restless legs (let me say that restless leg syndrome is a shit name for a diagnosis that isn't exclusively in the legs, just saying), I couldn't stop pacing around the house shaking my arms for more than six hours a night.

Blah blah blah, my lungs are okay now but I've never really recovered from that malarky.

The trauma from everything surrounding that event and my journey with tuberculosis was fucking shattering, and that's only some of the story. I've done my best not to think about it every day, but I do. This fucken whole COVID palaver has been absolutely terrifying, and seeing and hearing people get sick and struggle to breathe has really just been the scariest shit.

Every time I feel out of breath, feel a little twinge in my shoulder or any slight pain or abnormality anywhere in my body, when I watch a show with medical themes, if I think of visiting a hospital or going to a doctor – I often get light-headed and begin to feel deep, deep fear.

I am pissed off about what happened because a lot of things could have been avoided, particularly at the moment I was told what was going on for me was just asthma when it was something much more serious. It takes a lot for me to overcome the dread of talking to a doctor about my body because I am afraid of this happening again or being told I am going to die.

It's such an important thing to talk to doctors when you're not feeling well. Unfortunately, it will never not scare the shit out of me, but I am committed to working on it.

When it comes to surviving something brutal and painful, hearing that it should have made you heaps stronger is kinda the last fucken thing you wanna be told. When a scary and heavy thing happens to you it doesn't always make you stronger, it often traumatises the living fuck out of you and makes your anxiety worse. I will say at least I survived some of these things and am still here to have a whinge about shit sayings like this one. I reckon we can safely frisbee this old nonsense over the back fence and start again.

What doesn't kill you is a lot of things and some of them are shit, so hang in there!

FOCUS MORE

Cheers for that advice. I had no idea that all this time, all I had to do was just do it more to do it better.

Never been my strong suit, the old 'focus', nor has it been of any help when I'm reminded that I need to do it. I have a tidal wave of school report cards filled with words from my teachers demonstrating my ability to have very little focus/concentration.

Cop a go of one of my school report cards:

History: 37%
Nathanial [not how you spell my name, btw]
is a lively student who has great difficulty in
CONCENTRATING and following directions
in the classroom.

Geography: 43%
Nat has not made a promising start to his
Geographical studies. He must accept that hard work,
CONCENTRATION and application to his studies
in Geography are the ingredients for success.

Music: 48%
Nat is generally a positive member of class.
He often loses FOCUS and has to be reminded
to return to task. He works well when he
is interested and needs to develop a longer
CONCENTRATION span for necessary learning.

Personal Education: score N/A
He needs to FOCUS more on the task at hand in
both components of the subject.

English: 46%
[They used the word concentration four times
in this one!]
Nathaniel needs to show greater CONCENTRATION
and application of his work in English. His spelling
and vocabulary results have been quite poor
this semester, however in his last spelling test
he scored quite highly, showing that when he
CONCENTRATES on his work Nat can achieve good
results. CONCENTRATION in class should see Nat's
literature results improve as this was one area that
pulled his marks down considerably. Nat needs to
develop a bank of ideas that he can draw on for his
creative writing, as this was another area that let
him down. If Nat applies himself a little more and
CONCENTRATES in class, his results should improve
in the second semester.

Maths: 34%
[I obviously wasn't concentrating enough . . .]

Latin: 45%

Early in the term Nathaniel appeared to have difficulties settling down and FOCUSING on the work the class was doing.

Principal's note

The majority of Nat's marks are disappointing. While some of these low marks were caused because of the difficulty Nat has with written work, if he CONCENTRATED in class, listened carefully and put time into completing set tasks, he could gain better results.

I repeated that year.

Not surprised I repeated, to be honest. If you hate every second of school it doesn't exactly set you up for a massive lot of focused interest, and being told again and again that you're not doing it well enough doesn't help either. I think after a while I was so used to being shit at it and getting bad report cards I just assumed there was something wrong with me because I couldn't make the focus go.

Focus is one of those concepts that has always sounded real nice, but it really doesn't take much for me to not have any. I am so constantly stimulated by my surroundings and my thoughts that I can drift in and out of focus and conversation god knows how many times a minute. Really, to the point where I often sit still when someone's speaking to me, but in a flash I'm a million miles away, worried about the price of eggs in China and then if people can tell that I wasn't fully present and whether I've ruined everything, and then in a rush I'm back to the conversation at hand. I have to snap myself out of it constantly, and tell myself to focus on what the person right in front of me is saying. It rarely works.

I judge myself all the time for doing this, thinking shit like *Does it mean I'm self-involved?* I travel in annoying loops with it like some kind of roller-coaster where its self-perpetuating cycle bites its own tail as I try to hang on but then suddenly let go and end up flying out of my seat and over the fence. How the fuck is someone like me supposed to be able to sit through some long training session and take in important information when I'm clearly not wired for it? Even on planes when lives could be at stake, I drift off during the emergency evacuation demonstration. Like fuck, what if I'm sitting in an exit row where you get all the special extra talking-to by the cabin crew and you have to *really* not fucken miss the details? There's not even a test after the chat either. All that happens is they ask you whether you 'Got that?' or not. I of course say 'Yep' but in my head I'm like *What?*, just as I do to the other twenty conversations or people's names I can barely remember from today. I have a healthy 'wing it' approach to my life that has served me well in the past, so I suppose I'm resting easy on that fact. Plus, the instructions are next to the big red lever thing on the door so everything will be fine, right? Maybe I'll leaf through the safety card. Probably not; I'll most likely just fill myself with guilt later about the fact I could have jeopardised someone's life if the plane ride went to shit. I bet if it came to it and we all had to pile out in a hurry, I would be thinking about how I forgot the passenger's name next to me and feel like a gronk about that on top of panicking over whether the lever was supposed to be pulled up or down.

Is lack of focus an anxiety thing? Maybe it's my creative mind constantly searching for more shit to take the piss out of? Who the fuck knows. Probably a doctor.

I wonder what it's gonna take for me to stop and properly focus on something. An interest in the subject, I suppose. For example, I wrote this whole book, which took heaps of focus. I often get into a hyperfocus kinda zone when I find something really funny or when I'm playing music, cooking or even on stage at times. I suppose this stuff doesn't make me super anxious or I don't find it too difficult to get along with.

It should be said that it is near impossible to concentrate on something if you throw worrying into the mix, as worry will win every time. How the fuck am I supposed to focus while I think I'm dying? Sometimes my focus problems make me feel as though I'm trying to fly a kite in a tornado, with the shit whizzing all over the joint as

I keep hanging on hoping the fucken wind will chill out a bit and I'll remember where I parked the car. Having a phone with the internet on it has definitely made things a thousand times worse. Fuck, it can't be normal to have that much info driven through your brain at that pace, yet my brain loves it, particularly when I'm anxious or struggling to concentrate on something. It feels like I'm chewing on my own brain when I doomscroll through a ton of opinions, shows, jokes, news, pictures and memes. I feel exhausted and kinda hungover if I do it for too long. Definitely a shit idea, but I do it anyway.

I see these apps to help you calm your mind, promising to bring a sense of mindfulness to your day, reduce anxiety levels and improve sleep. I try them occasionally, but to be honest I get so fucken frustrated and bored so fast 'cause I can't focus on the slow-paced calming bit. I become so annoyed that I'm not focusing on not focusing that I don't focus even more. You could argue that meditation is perfect for someone like me, whereas I would argue that it is simultaneously the worst shit ever. I started doing it on a recommendation from a mate of mine who also happens to be an amazing doctor. I very occasionally go through these periods of being so profoundly fucken anxious I feel like I'm on another planet for weeks and sometimes months on end. It's fucked. I get kinda light-headed and feel fogged out for fucken ages; once I had it for eight months in a row, actually during the time I started making cooking videos when COVID was kicking off in the middle of a bushfire – no surprises there! The fuck ton of traumatic sleep disturbances I enjoy from my restless leg syndrome makes it heaps more hectic. What I have learnt is that trying to calm the fuck down helps, so I try shit to help . . . like meditation.

The problem is, asking my head to shut up is like waving a red flag in front of a bull: it loves the attention and will run for it when it gets spooked. Maybe not the best analogy, but it's kind of what happens. I have persevered with meditation, though. Well, I have turned up to it anyway. Whether I've achieved anything like a meditative state I'm not sure, but I clocked on for the job plenty of times.

I have been to a few meditation courses where they teach you to shut the fuck up in your brain. I always feel like a massive traitor, sitting there while someone rings a little bell and you all just shhhhhhhh now. It drives me absolutely fucking mad to have to sit still for more than 60 seconds, but I fucken do it! I managed to keep it up for a few months at one point. Most of the people on the course fucked off but I didn't, which made me proud of myself for a hot minute. That's how desperate I was for the anxiety to stop. I think there were close to thirty people in the class when it started and by the end there were only seven of us. Like a kind of meditation *Survivor*: 'Who will think about scratching their bum first?' 'Who will get voted off by their own mind?'

It's not easy to face your brain head-on ... hang on, what? Facing my brain head? I should say that I typed 'brain' as 'Brian' just then and it made me laugh.

Said with fist in the air: 'I have finally faced my Brian head-on, everyone!' *

I'm kind of proving my point here, really. Anyway, it was hard – really hard – to not just let out a massive sigh or fart or scratch my nose or god forbid go for a mid-meditation piss. At times I felt held hostage by the whole thing but I knew it was important to keep trying, not that it was made easy by a few environmental factors, let me say. Some of the hardest parts were just sitting cross-legged on a hard, wooden floor – they did say some people could lie down or sit in chairs but it felt like a trap, a test maybe, to see if you needed training wheels. For sure, if I had taken the most inviting one, to lie down, I would either fall asleep or look weak in front of the other meditators. Really, I'm just a stupid dickhead who should have taken the chair at least, given that my back was fucking killing me. But if you take the chair then the whole class is sitting on the ground and you look like a fuckwit who's not taking it seriously, 2 feet above everyone.

---

* gets kicked out of meditation class.

But that wasn't even the worst thing – seriously, it was how fucken hot the fucken room was – like at least give me a running start here, a bit of air con? It wasn't like the course was super cheap either; I felt that in turning up to a class to do fuck-all I could at least ask for a bit of temperature management. The real kick in the guts was that I saw there even was an air con unit on the wall, but they just had the fucken doors open to the 35-degree heat. Fuck me, I couldn't stop sweating with back pain, which of course meant that I sat there contemptuous of the fact they wouldn't just crank the air and let me lie down like a baby. I feel like this was a set-up: is it a part of the test? Like, can't 'no air con' be the end of semester exam? I don't have a great history of coming out ahead at the end of term but at least let me practise in a temperature that's not peak Australian summer sun. Fuck, the more I think about it the more I remember struggling with the course; even in the foyer before the meditation, everyone was talking so quietly,

though the meditation hadn't started yet. I feel so put upon by quiet at times, particularly when it's not necessary. But ya gotta try to go with the flow, right?

To be perfectly honest, I learnt pretty much nothing from the three months that I went to that one, but I'm glad I gave it a crack. I did eventually stop feeling as bad as I had earlier, but I'd overthought every part of it so much by that point it was hard to prove what it was I was doing in my life that was the factor that actually helped.

Ya gotta give 'getting better' a crack; it's always worth it even if it doesn't pan out in the long run and gives you the shits. Fuck knows there's a boatload of nonsense out there that works really well for some people and not for others. I have tried heaps of weird shit and most of it hasn't hit the spot, but what it has done is given me some good stories to carry on about, and I love talking shit, so there's that.

Lacking concentration on certain stuff may come off rude or ignorant at times, but what are ya gonna do? Pretend concentrate? That is not a good look, and it has a high rate of getting busted doing it. I have found that saying, 'Shit, sorry, could you say that again?' or fessing up to feeling anxious has helped even the keel, and while it can feel a bit socially jarring it's often only momentary and can help calm the vibe enough to have a chance to really actually focus on what's going on. That sometimes works for me but might not be accessible for you.

'I FEEL SO PUT UPON BY QUIET AT TIMES.'

It does have to make you wonder how I wrote a book, hey? I think it's because I probably feel more in control of my environment when I get a chance to express my thoughts in this way, maybe? When I'm not in my own familiar spaces I tend to feel a little scrambled, like everything needs something from me in a way. I probably don't have to scan the room for shit to distract me like a fucken disobedient terminator, but I do.

I reckon I will get better at concentrating as the years go on, or maybe I'll just master bullshitting that I know what we were all talking about just then, and avoid repeatedly reintroducing myself to everyone. Don't give yourself a hard time for not being a Zen master at concentrating. Anxiety and focus are not good mates at all, and neither are mid-summer meditation and no air con – just sayin'.

STAY
IN
SCHOOL

First of all I will acknowledge that education is super vital and important shit, and I think I was truly lucky to be able to receive an education . . . or some of one, at least. I was just bad at it.

The advice to 'stay in school' is an old one, suggesting overall that rather than running amok in the streets, you knuckle down and get an education. That bit mostly makes sense to me, plus if I was a parent (which I'm not), I would no doubt opt for the safer option for my kid every time. And trying to homeschool and work a paying job at the same time? Punishing. Let alone if you are a single parent trying to care for a young person and have time to do anything else at all, then phwoar, bravo.

Let's be clear, when I hang shit on the saying 'stay in school' – which I will – I'm most certainly not talking about early education here, which is absolutely fucken necessary. If you let most kids do what they wanted instead of going to school it would be total fucken chaos. The streets would be rife with lolly-filled demons on scooters, every shopping mall filled to the brim with loitering freeloaders surviving off complimentary Gloria Jeans samples and driving all of the retail staff mad with pretend shopping like an eternal school holiday. The amount of screen time alone that would be consumed would cause a major spike in global power usage and the climate crisis would accelerate at such breathtaking velocity that we would all be under water by the end of the year.

Fuck, I remember moments of feeling so hard done by as a kid. I would act like such a grumpy little ratbag when I wasn't allowed to just swan about and do what I wanted. Of course, you can't let children do whatever they want because it won't end well. I have vivid memories of wishing I could watch TV or play video games for eternity – anything not to go to school. I fantasised like nothing else that I could just stay home and do what I wanted instead of going to a place filled with boring work. Shit, if you had let me eat whatever I wanted as a child it would have without a doubt been a diet strictly consisting of literally the lowest health-star-rated foods possible: nuggets and lollies would have been flying into my body so quickly I'd have barely had time to breathe. Then I would have probably watched all the MA 15+ and R-rated movies I wasn't allowed to see, scared the shit out of myself and burnt the fucken house down trying to make hot chips on the stove.

At least that's what I reckon I would have done.

While that would be fun for a few weeks, it's not the road to a happy adult life. Nor is it what I think this 'stay in school' line is actually crapping on about.

It's hard to know the reason for going to shit-boring school when you're young, 'cause it is more or less exactly that: boring. What's even worse is you're supposed to stay at school until you work out what you want to 'do' with your life. How the fuck are you supposed to know what you want to do in life at any age, particularly when you're young?

When I say what to 'do' I suppose I mean pick a career. Interesting that, hey? When people kick off conversation with someone new, often one of the first things you're asked is, 'What do you do?' Pretty fucken tough one to answer when you're not sure, or maybe don't have work at the moment. Maybe you fucken hate your job and don't want to identify with it. That's fair, I have had plenty of jobs where I have wanted to be associated with just about anything else as a person than the job title of 'picker packer' or 'cold caller'. While I think it's okay to enjoy a strong sense of identity from your work, I think it's equally okay not to. Maybe what you call your 'work' doesn't pay you anything? Is that still what you 'do'?

I think so.

Money far from defines the value of people as humans, and the amount you make doesn't mean your answer to 'What do you do?' is more important than anyone else's.

What if you're simply Saz or Vince? What if that's the answer to what you 'do'? You just live as Saz or Vince. I reckon that's actually fucken

super great, and what's more, totally fine as a life goal, particularly if you're happy.

The pressure to be a super successful Saz or Vince comes from everyone else most of the time. Maybe you're content with having zero idea what's coming next or what your fucken five-year plan is. Fucken love it! It's gotta be all about the search for some kind of happiness in the end, surely? Believe it or not, but some people's happiness doesn't include the smash-hits bangers that are owning a house, having kids and slaving away at a job that pays 100 k or more a year.

This is where I feel a lot of the pressure to 'stay in school' comes from – the idea is that if you stay in school and learn more about more shit then it opens doors for you blah blah blah. While that can be true for some people, it's not always the point. The pressure to know what you wanna do and be as an adult is huuuge. Where's the cut-off for 'should know what you want to do by now'? Age twelve? Seventeen? Twenty-five? I've had a few deadlines thrown at me, all of which are fucken nonsense. I've also heard a few people say, 'Some people never work out what they want to do!' And I would hundy believe that. I am lucky that I knew I wanted to be a noisy pain in the arse from a young age, but it was hard to know what qualification you are supposed to get to make you a shoo-in for that gig.

I stayed in school until the beginning of Year 11 and then when the rhetoric of 'You know you don't have to be here?' sank in enough, I was fucken off like a shot faster than you could say 'Fuck this shit'. I had repeated a year at school, which, fuck me, is the worst news to hear as a kid who already fucken hates the place. I muscled through the days and weeks and years 'til I had a way out.

Overall, I didn't do well at school. All my grades were more or less dogshit – some of them were okay at times – but for the most part it was becoming a bit of a joke my staying there. Mind you, it wasn't helped by the fact I was a really messed-up kid. I had some tricky family issues, having left a hectic church lifestyle with a lot of severe mental health problems, which made everything in life profoundly harder than it needed to be at that age. I spent a lot of heavy time lost in my head, crying, sometimes screaming in desperation, and there were lots of moments of rocking back and forth mumbling to myself, not knowing what to do with the universe. Things were not fucken good, mate. I tried medications to see if they would help. I self-medicated with other things which, while it was a fun escape at times, in truth made everything a hundred times worse. Going to school during my teens was the worst fucken headache while wrestling with all this drama going on in my life. I had no idea what the fuck the future was gonna look like AT ALL.

I did try to 'stay in school' and go to uni to study music once I'd left during Year 11, but really that was just a distraction to stop me from becoming a massive party wreck, which I kinda did anyway. It wasn't all bad. I had some great experiences at college or uni or whatever ya wanna call it. I met some close friends who I still love very dearly to this day . . . well, pretty much just one, actually, but Harry is like having a room full of mates in one person, so it counts.

I wanted to be a rock star so kept telling myself that was gonna happen. What I really wanted was to be on stage. I never especially cared what the circumstances of that would be, much to the annoyance of many an open mic attendee or partygoer. For as long as I can remember I've wanted to perform and make people laugh, and while that is a fantastic-sounding idea, it doesn't make you a whole lot of actual livable income if you're not a 'professional' or haven't realised what it means as actual employment. This is what I hated about my dream, that it wasn't going to make me any fast money. It's super great being superglued to your dreams of being successful, but when you've got a head full of self-loathing, mental health issues and marijuana smoke, the outlook is a little grim.

I fucken prattled on about this in my first book. I also shudder at the idea that this is gonna read like some kind of 'I made it work, so can youuu' punish of a read. God knows my advice should be taken with a grain of salt, I'm just filled with unrequested opinions of my own on the matter. I think what I'm trying to convey is that I fucken had no idea what the fuck I was gonna do other than have consecutive meltdowns after I left school. If I had stayed, would that have helped? Probably not. Am I going to keep answering my own questions in this book? Looks like it.

Some advice suits some people more than others. Staying in a place that's making you feel like shit about yourself and not teaching you anything is gonna start having the opposite effect after a while, I reckon. Who gives a shit if you don't know what you wanna do? Fuck, the pressure to KNOW straight away what you're gonna be in society's eyes for the rest of your entire life is so much for the brain of a young person or really anyone's brain that barely knows what day it is, let alone one that is dealing with all the social and existential pressures of the day to day. Some people never work out what they want to do for employment or spend years working at a career that they now hate, probably 'cause they aren't super excited to work in general and have other goals in life that aren't delivering stupid shit to your house. I think the decision to bail on a gig and try something else is admirable, although not easy by any means.

Having a job is great and all, but there are a lot of them out there and hey, maybe most of them aren't for you. Maybe you're not well enough to be able to work at the moment. Or the idea of being in a place with people you don't know plugging away together at a thing you all hate doing sounds like a panic attack waiting to happen. Fair enough, it probably is. I've hated almost every job I've ever had – not all of them, but a lot. I personally have felt quite out of place with the whole standard-issue:

Leave school
Get a job
Get married
Cop a mortgage
Have kids
Retire

I knew that path would just make me fucking miserable.

There is so much pressure on people to become the thing they're told they have to be, and all within an annoyingly specific time window. Is the whole point that you're supposed to be able to make at least enough money to buy your own land and retire on it to finally relax and enjoy life, but not before you pay for a bunch of ratbag kids to do the same? Each to their own for sure, but with what my gut reckons, I think I might give most of that a miss, and I might not be alone in thinking that.

I do have the habit of being a bit anti-the-normal-pants about everything, so I guess that's my shit – I just hate the idea that someone is out there giving themselves a hard time for not being enough for the world around them. People love you whether you're a firefighter, doctor, scientist, broke musician, tattooist, artist, poet, support worker or an out-of-work punk. If someone wants to hurry you up about it, I reckon flip 'em a digit and tell them to get fucked. While there is a clear benefit for some people to spend a lot of time studying, maybe it's not for you.

But hey, if you're keen to become a doctor or nurse, I mean, we would be pretty fucked without medics around, so thank you for the sacrifices you'll make to get there.

Take your time to work out what ya wanna bloody 'do', and if you need something to fill the gap in an intimidating conversation with a very important employed person who has an attitude about people being otherwise, tell them you're on a secret mission and can't talk about it yet.

I have spent many years of my life unemployed for one or more reasons and at times have found myself meeting someone's parents or a successful person where very quickly I'm on the receiving end of the 'What do you do?' question. It always immediately sent me into a panic, particularly when getting hammered was the only thing I'd done that week.

So I thought I might riff on a few ideas here to help get you out of a tricky spot called 'Job titles with no actual job'. Here are some suggestions you could say you 'do':

1. ARTIST

While it doesn't instantly win you the respect of the dad
who works in finance, it's hard to prove that you're not one,
so when inevitably asked, 'What kind of art?' you can say
'postmodern', quickly google 'bent fork', show them
a picture of that, they won't get it, and BOOM. Artist.

2. CRYPTO

I'm not convinced anyone really knows what the fuck
is going on with crypto anyway, so you should be home
and free quick smart.

3. DATA ENTRY

Technically you're not lying if you ever use a phone to text
anyone. Congrats, you just got yourself a data entry job
without even knowing.

4. DRIVER

If you don't have a licence this will be hard to prove,
but if you've driven a car before, even if only once in your
life, then you can say you're a driver. 'For who, Uber?'
Your answer can be 'Depends on the job'.

5. CONSULTANT

What do you need to know? Let me take it offline and
I'll circle back.

6. TECH SUPPORT

For your uncle probs, who's struggling to get his iPad to work after accidentally doing a factory reset.

7. FREELANCER

And constantly waiting for payment works well as an excuse for being broke, too.

9. INTERIOR DESIGNER

Rearranged your bedroom once, right?

10. GARDENER

Pulled a weed or two? Done.

So whether you've grown up in the school of hard knocks (which to me sounds like a school where you bang your head a lot) or have done well in an actual school, who you are as a person isn't reliant on the marks you got in school or the ones you're gonna get later. Ya don't always kick the ball straight between the posts in life, 'cause sometimes you kick the fucken footy into a table of drinks, then have to replace those drinks and maybe end up laughing about it with the people whose drinks you had to replace, and now you have a bunch of new friends all because you tried to kick a ball . . .

I dunno, something like that.

Party on!

EVERYTHING HAPPENS FOR A REASON

EVERYTHING!

Happens for what reason, eh?

Are these wise words supposed to help me digest what I just went through? This saying is mostly a piss-poor effort at trying to help by throwing the towel in, rather than suggesting 'Let's talk about shit' and try to make stuff better. It's well-meaning and all that, but so is a bunch of other old crap that doesn't suit the modern-day person. From where I'm sitting it seems more escapist than of any usable help in a real-life tough moment.

It all happens for a reason hey? Why? Because the 'universe' has planned my future and it's just part of this week's programming, so get on board, apparently.

Heads up, this one really shits me so I'm gonna get fucken stuck in. You were warned, or it was just supposed to beeeeeeeee.

I suppose it could be nice, just to sit back and relax and let fate do its worst because life has all just been pre-planned in some weird meeting for you – except the bit where it all took place without you there; that part is somewhat rude. This saying is dressed up in many different ways that actually mean the same exact fucking thing, whether it's called 'luck' or maybe it was your 'karma' or even 'serendipity' that this and that should all have happened – but was it?

It's all planned out, hey? Are we allowed to see the manila folder with all our personal info and pre-planned activities in it, so we know exactly what we're in for? Who do you speak to about this? Do you reckon you would even wanna see it if you had the chance? I mean, if you believe in it so much, why not, right? Or does that ruin the surprise?

I'd love to know what the reason was for me losing my passport, for example. Was that to teach me to look after my shit better? Is it because Fate hates travelling to Thailand this time of year and would prefer that I flew at a later Fateful date? Is there a cheaper flight I'm unaware of? But hang on! The replacement cost of the passport is more than the savings from the reduced price of the flight. Gee whizz, I'm so confused. *

Or how about the fact that the apartments I rent keep leaking like a fucken sieve, is that Fate? Is it my Fate to argue with a strata over whether or not I left the fucken window open during a storm every time it rains, as if I love having the carpet all wet like some fucken goblin has set up a slip n slide out of mould?

'DO WHATEVER MAKES YA HAPPY AND DON'T LET FATE BULLY YOU INTO THINKING YOU HAVE NO CHOICE.'

* slaps forehead.

Do I put my foot up on the edge of the now-wet couch and yell, 'I am Sir Fates-A-Lot of the Damp Table and having my card skimmed and bank account drained on rent day was my destinyyyyyyy'?

Question: what is the meaning of all of this nonsense?

Answer: it's for a predetermined reason but you're not allowed to know 'cause then you could learn from it and that would mean life is rigged. Suck it up.

It's such a fucken weak-cup-of-tea explanation of existence. I can have a far more profound existential crisis than losing a passport or taking my chances on rental roulette, thank you very much.

Have you ever done something that was a bloody lot of hard work or cost a fucking tonne of money that you worked really hard to earn, just to find out that it went to shit or didn't make you happy in the way you'd planned? What the fuck was the point of expending all that energy, huh? Oh, 'cause reasons, okay sure – great explanation.

So let's say Donna has spent months building this tiny model ship inside a glass bottle. It's been a true journey of passion, patience and effort. Every little part had to be meticulously glued with a fucken tiny stick through the tiny hole at the end of the bottle. It is something Donna is really proud of, something she should absolutely be very proud of. She worked on it for hours after work every day; in fact, all her spare time goes into making these tiny ships in bottles. She is good at it, it represents something other than the crushing mundanity of everyday life. She loves how it brings her a sense of contentment. Though it's complicated work, it's always worth the hours it takes to craft these incredible feats of patience and skill.

Donna works an office job for a real estate agent who is a fucken piece of shit of a boss who blames Donna almost daily for pretty much everything, even when things are his fault. He yells at her if the photocopier is jammed 'cause the rollers are old and damaged since he refuses to spend any money repairing them because he seemingly enjoys being an arsehole more than being a problem-solver. Even when the water fountain's little blue cold tap wasn't producing cold enough water he would ask Donna, 'Why the fuck is the water coming out of this tap the same temperature as the other fucken one? Did you do something to it, Donna?' Donna loathes her boss, but the pay is decent and it's close to where she lives. Though she hates her job, Donna daydreams about sailing away on one of the tiny ships she's

been building, fantasising about happier times, imagining one day she may even sail to somewhere exotic on an amazing old ship.

On the night Donna finally finishes her latest tiny ship in a bottle she's just over the moon with how it's looking. Every, little, bit . . . perfect! Donna loves it and it makes her smile so much that she allows herself to wonder. Maybe if she brought her finished model ship into work to keep on her desk it would give her a little dose of joy when the days were otherwise filled with tension and stress. So, the next day she places it proudly on top of her desk, looking at it every now and then and smiling. *This was a great idea*, Donna thinks.

That is, of course, until the boss comes past and sees Donna's handiwork for the first time. He proceeds to grab it and squint at it, holding it up high against the office's fluorescent lighting, asking loudly, 'How the fuck do they do this shit, ya reckon? How do they get the ship into the fucken bottle thing?' as he shakes it violently, trying to work it out, 'cause he is an idiot.

Donna says with urgency, 'Could you please be careful. It took me a long time to make that!'

The boss replies, 'Fuck off, you made this shit?'

'Yes, it's taken me a lot of hours over many weeks to make that one.'

The boss, looking unimpressed, then exclaims, 'Maybe if you put as much effort into your work here at the office, we would all own a fucken boat hahahahaha!' He's holding his chest, laughing and coughing so hard that his fingers slip and he drops Donna's tiny ship onto the floor. It smashes into a thousand pieces.

Donna is left utterly heartbroken.

Question: what is the meaning of all this nonsense?

Answer: it's for a mysterious, predetermined reason. Suck it up.

'I'M THE PERSON WITH A LOUD MOUTH WHO CAN'T JUST LEAVE IT ALONE, AND I LOVE PULLING EVERYTHING APART BECAUSE THAT'S HOW MY BRAIN WORKS.'

I'll tell ya what the reason is: the boss is a massive shithead who doesn't give a rat's arse about anyone except himself. But in my mind that's hardly an explanation for *every*thing happening for a reason. Was it Donna's destiny to have to deal with her chode of a boss being an absolute loser? Why did it have to take that much heartache and struggle for her to realise she should probably leave that awful job? Why does Fate get all the credit? Seems very unfair to me.

If you're religious, then I get why that concept of everything happening for a reason works for you. Living for a higher being and believing that good and bad stuff have a place in your god's plan can be a comfort. But if you're not religious, you're likely looking for a meaning to life and an explanation as to why all this shit keeps happening to the world. There is so much heavy shit going down on this planet and it's hard to accept that much of it is because of us humans, rather than the magical 'reason'. Where does this leave our own responsibility for the goings-on of the world, if it seems to be able to take a back seat to Fate?

Who am I to say that bad stuff isn't all happening for a reason? Well, I'm the person with a loud mouth who can't just leave it alone, and I love pulling everything apart because that's how my brain works. I don't have any qualifications as a life explainer/coach/mentor/philosopher, but I do have all of the anxiety in the world and a fistful of issues I'd love to fucken blame something or someone for, but can't. The likelihood is that life just is what it is and I have to suffer in my jocks and make the best of it.

Don't get me wrong, I don't think there is anything bad about looking for meaning in the tough or positive experiences life throws at us – there is certainly a shitload of lessons to learn along the way – but nor do I think they're all happening for some fucken predetermined reason. Of course, the cause and effect of events are very literal explanations of why something happened. Take, for example, your decision to spend your first time trying to ice skate in shorts instead of pants. That's the *reason* you are not only cold but also the *reason* you've lacerated your unprotected knees and are now bleeding all over the Macquarie Centre ice rink.

Looking for a reason behind everything or kicking back and letting destiny call the shots takes the fun out of the party and takes away your ability to have chipped in to the next life move. Fixating over the reason you ended up at the park on a Thursday and saw a brown dog walking past a brown car while listening to James Brown doesn't actually mean anything particularly special is happening other than you've experienced a coincidence, unless you're Keanu Reeves in *The Matrix*, because in that case it's a glitch and you're in big trouble. RUN!

I think it's fine to believe whatever you want about anything you fucken want as long as you're not demanding your unproven theory to be taken as fact by everyone else, telling me that it's my destiny to suffer certain things, people and places. After all, there's an innocent sweetness to imagination and wanting things to be okay, and in seeking out meaning in all the crazy rides that life takes us on. I think if some event or moment feels profoundly meaningful to you then it's exactly that: profound. It holds a particular significance for you and that's what matters. If you're on board with the idea that Fate is in charge of these outcomes, then by all means go for more of that stuff.

I had a moment as a kid when I was riding my bike down a street in Sydney where every house's fence on each side was Federation-style wrought iron with a spiked fleur-de-lis decoration along the top. I was cycling home while trying to hang on to a skateboard at the same time. The reason I mention the spiked fences is that I was riding the bike with no hands (something I was quite good at, or was I?) which was a bad idea given that these fences were death wishes for any cyclist in the neighbourhood. My wheel hit something and I flew off the bike and smacked my *neck* right onto the fence outside a house ...

... THE ONLY FUCKEN FENCE THAT DIDN'T HAVE SPIKES ON IT! It was a flat metal fence.

It still gave me a massive scrape up my neck but at least it didn't have a fence post going through it, hey? So was it Fate that I didn't fucken die from being fenced through the neck? Some would say – *I* would say – that I got really fucken lucky that day that I didn't kill myself by being a dickhead.

It's tough hearing that Fate and destiny could be determining my life because it makes me feel as though I have no control over my own existence and that some unknown arsehole is just flooring it at full speed towards more nonsense I'm unprepared for. Can't it be simply because life goes on and shit happens? Lots of factors change the outcome of other factors and a lot of those factors are within your power to influence much of the time. For example, you may choose to eat only a diet of dried fruit and cayenne pepper milkshakes for a week. What's likely to happen next is that you spend the whole fucken week on the dunny.

That's not fate, that's because you were eating like an absolute fuckwit and now your life has changed course due to you making a very deliberate decision.

'I DON'T THINK THERE IS ANYTHING BAD ABOUT LOOKING FOR MEANING IN THE TOUGH OR POSITIVE EXPERIENCES LIFE THROWS AT US.'

Maybe a gross example but nonetheless: my point is, it's not *The Truman Show*.

You are of course limited to your means in certain moments and some people are in much luckier and easier spots to sway the needle in favour of their ideal outcome, due to money, privilege, education etc. but being told that it's all happened for a preordained reason will never not shit me.

I simply don't wanna buckle up and let Fate take over because I reckon we are way more dynamic than what our wheel of fortune has to offer.

Question: what is the meaning of all of this nonsense?

Answer: actually, sometimes shit happens 'cause shit just sucks but equally, good shit happens and your day can turn out to be a ripper too. I reckon definitely do whatever makes ya happy and don't let Fate bully you into thinking you have no choice or influence.

Not everything has to happen for a reason . . .

. . . unless the reason is YOUUUUUUUUUUU.*

---

*   cue Hoobastank's 'The Reason'.

t's a big call.

You neck that fifth glass of thingo, flick your hair back, bite your bottom lip and let a few spicy leg kicks rrrrrrrip, followed by rapidly moving in several drunken, under-rehearsed ways in front of a group of strangers. What can possibly go wrong?

I feel complex emotions about this one. Let me explain where I'm at with it all.

First up, don't get me wrong here: I don't want to pooh-pooh the joy of dancing. It is one of the great freeing moments in life, and I think you should absolutely go for it when you feel the inner boogie coming on, particularly when a banger of a track is playing. I think it's really sweet seeing someone having a little solo groove with their headphones on at the bus stop or on the walk home. It always makes me smile and think *fucken champion* – I soak up a little positive energy from it. It's a true moment of self-expression that you should have permission to kick off at just about any time in life.

However, I know not everyone is in the mood to bust out some sick moves all the time, which is why being encouraged to do so when you don't want to is fucken annoying and can cause high levels of stress. The whole 'Awww come onnnnnn, come dance with us' routine when you're feeling socially anxious is absolutely fucken terrifying, particularly if you're not the dancing type, a little body conscious, have a fear of public humiliation or want the turbo person who is breathing energy drink and vodka in your face to fuck off. Not to mention if your parents are there . . . God, take me away from that scene!

As someone who lives with quite intense generalised anxiety, the phrase 'dance like no one is watching' is riddled with danger, and by the way 'no one is watching' is not how anxiety works: in your mind everyone is watching all the time, whether that's even true or not. Yet I have danced like no one was watching many times in fact, and while I don't have a huge complex about my dancing it has definitely become more calculated and restrained over the years. I've certainly had some overly brave and sometimes alcohol-fuelled moments on the dance floor I'd love to forget – who hasn't, right? There're a few events where I really let myself fucken go for it and pulled my fair share of wild and passionate dance moves, some previously unseen by the human eye even, some embarrassing the clogs off me so hard I had to go for a private self-analysis session in the bathroom afterwards to calm down. Alcohol has a lot to answer for here. Ever wondered why people dance at weddings so much? Booze!

The problems with drinking can be listed 1000 ways, but in respect to cutting a rug it has been the dickhead friend who's given many a person a licence to kill on the D-floor when they probably should have suggested you sit down and not go for the high kick in cowboy boots because now you're on your arse and don't feel like dancing anymore.

Okay, I think this book is about to have unqualified dance lessons in it.

Great.

Before we begin, can I just say how fucken weird it is to encourage someone to do something that very clearly makes them uncomfortable, all for your selfish enjoyment? It's gross and doesn't even make sense unless you're a psychopath. If you want people to dance with you that badly, go to a dance class or maybe pour yourself a tall glass of chill the fuck out.

Anyway.

Let's put ourselves at the most classic place where you're expected to be pressured into dancing: the infamous drunken wedding.

Not everyone feels like dancing all the time and you may find yourself in this scenario from time to time, so I'm here to help.

Straight outta the gate, here's a set of non-dance moves for those of you who don't feel like dancing:

1. THE 'BULLSHIT PAIN TWO-STEP'

Tried and true and no one can argue or disprove it, not that you should have to argue about dancing, but given the situation, a quickfire 'Aw thanks, but my back is pretty crook' with a hand on your back should have you doing fuck-all in no time. And if the arsehole won't let it go then they just look like a dickhead to everyone around them and you now have something to talk about at the table. Boom.

2. THE 'DRINK FINISHER'

I mean, trying to dance and drink at the same time? Very unsafe indeed, and if anyone asks you to do that, call the cops (not really). A quick gesture with your drink and 'I'll just finish this up and see ya out there', followed by a nod to the dance floor should defuse the situation in no time flat. Keep filling that bad boi back up and voila, you're off the hook.

3. THE 'SORRY I'VE GOTTA TAKE THIS'

A quick pretend chatty on the blower is like cementing a brick wall around yourself that says Do Not Disturb, which is exactly what you're chasing in this moment. Make sure you turn that shit onto airplane mode or you might get caught out faking a phone call and could be doing the nutbush and crying inside.

4. THE 'CATCH-UP'

This is one of Jules' faves: 'Haven't seen [insert guest name] in ages, just catching up and I'll see ya there in a bit.' What a cracker, it has the dance floor fisherman casting their line in another pond so fast you'll think you're watching Rex Hunt.

5. THE '360-DEGREE THANKS, I HATE IT'

This is the handbrake of moves if you know you're in for a real bulldozer of an arsehole who isn't likely to let it go. It's not the most accessible of the bunch, I'll agree, but it will work with enough conviction behind it. Just let the punisher know 'I actually really hate dancing, but thank you'. It's not only weird and unexpected but should also scramble the enemy's brains enough for them to search elsewhere. It really should pull the rug right out from underneath them and destroy any counterargument they might have. If for some reason they say 'Awww you don't mean that', just get your best stern face on and say, 'I really do actually, but you go on'. That should work.

But hey, maybe you *do* in fact wanna join the dance floor but don't have any real solid dance moves in the bank? That's okay, you don't have to be Michael Flatley's Lord of the Dance to join in. A little head-nod to the beat will get you out of trouble.

In my opinion, there are plenty of tired and strange moves that I do think need to take a back seat. I can hear some of you out there asking, 'Nat, who are you to be giving textual dance lessons?'

Well listen here, champion! I did a few street dancing lessons at a community hall when I was about eight or ten years old, *and* I did the robot at my Year 6 formal so I think I know what I'm talking about, okay? To be honest those so-called street dancing lessons serve more to embarrass me than help a lot of the time, but whatever.

Dancing is like riding a bike: just get on, remove the training wheels and get your uncle to push you down a metaphorical hill of dancing until you're cutting a two-wheeled rug so mean that people are asking if you're a professional.

But as I was saying before you interrupted me with your hypothetical question, in my travels I've noticed a few overused moves that can be quite confronting, particularly with several drinks behind them.

Here is my top ten list of moves I try to avoid:

1. THE MR BEAN THRUST

If you're partial to mimicking old mate Mr Bean, I think you have to stop and ask yourself, what are you doing with your body right now? This is a truly problematic dusty cupboard of a move for obvious reasons, I would have thought. And it's made much worse if you're wearing a tie that's bouncing off your pelvis like some kind of limp fish-and-chip-shop's plastic ribboned doorway. Do I really need to explain why this is a bad idea? Randomly thrusting at someone with your arms dead straight and a bottom-lip-bitten look on your face is super bad news for everyone else trying to dance around you. It's quite a bizarre body language conversation to be having with anyone, let alone with a group of people dancing together. It's less of a dance move and comes off as more of a threat . . . a truly creepy addition to any routine.

2. RAISE THE ROOF

Unless you want to apply for a new development application you're gonna have to leave the roof at the height it is. While this 'pushing your arms away from yourself' move is not really an issue as such, it often comes with an out of time shot-put at the ceiling bobbing motion, and if this is the only one you're deploying in the name of dance, your arms are gonna get tired fast. Can I recommend throwing in a dip, a spin and a clap to keep this one fresh and give your body some variety?

3. POINTING AT PEOPLE

Have we learnt nothing? Pointing is rude. Why are you pointing at me and staring me down? It's also quite loud at this wedding, which is adding to the stress of it all.

Maybe swap the finger guns move to a more cowboy-style vibe, let off a few pretend rounds at the sky and then holster those weapons.

4. ONE-HANDED POINT AT THE SKY WITH BONUS SINGLE FOOT TAP

If it's a Midnight Oil covers band, I'll let this one slide, otherwise . . . You're pointing again: rude.

5. THE KICKBOXER

Listen tough guy, this shit is straight-up annoying. It's not a hardcore music gig, and even if it was, it's *still* annoying. If you want to fight someone, go to an MMA gym or some shit. No one wants to get Jackie Chan'd to the face while they're trying to have a good time, so drop the spin kicks, Terry.

6. THE THUMBS-UP

While I appreciate a good thumbs-up as much as the next person, too much of a good thing is often not a good thing. Coupla fucken thumbs with a scooped hip and dip I am in support of for sure, but don't let it take the wheel for too long otherwise it looks like you're giving everyone the 'well done, champ' too much.

7. HIP BUMP

I think we can agree that the COVID-19 pandemic has changed the landscape for dance floors across the world for the last few years, and while things have begun to relax a little, this far from warrants you smashing your arse into me in celebration. As they say, it takes two to tango, and a solo hip bump is like a solo tango, if you catch my drift.

8. HIGH-FIVE SEARCHING

I love that you're having a good time but this is not the moment for high-fives. Walking around constantly pressuring people into giving you a high-five on the dance floor is not a good look. Maybe when the song or evening has ended then sure. Until then, keep your notes in ya wallet, Richie Rich.

9. HANDS-ON-HIPS GYRATION

The Macarena is not something I have happy memories of, mainly from being made to do it on repeat in primary school. One part of that dance involved putting your hands on your hips and gyrating. The idea that this will ever happen again outside of that cringey part of my life fills me with dread. Please take it outside and do it in the shed on your own.

10. THE HEY HEY IT'S 'MY HANDS IN YOUR FACE' SATURDAY

Yes, I can see you. You're hard to miss, to be honest, while you wave your hands at me as if you've saved me a seat. We aren't sitting down and this manoeuvre is taking up a lot of space on the dance floor. Waving your hands in the air like you just don't care should be used with care, and should be like a cherry on the top of the Cut a Rug Sundae rather than the 'heaps of sauce' bit.

If you don't agree with what I've said here I think that's fair. Maybe you love some or all of these moves and dancing represents a great time to you, no matter who's around you. I think dancing is a wonderful freeing thing and I also think it's awesome if you're the kind of person who can get among a boogie without feeling the anxiety of it all. People are working with varying levels of ability and passion, however, and might feel a little intimidated by it, so I think it's important to talk about options.

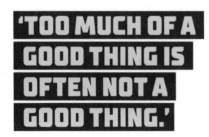

'TOO MUCH OF A GOOD THING IS OFTEN NOT A GOOD THING.'

Dancing is relative, and it can be tricky to muster the courage to do any. Feeling up for it is hard for a lot of people, particularly anxious people. So when someone says 'dance like no one is watching' I feel like they are speaking to themselves more than to me – if you don't wanna dance or aren't in the mood then I say: don't.

I'm comfortable with pretty much whatever it takes to make yourself feel okay to shake a leg at. But I know that people *are* watching and that's why I don't want to right now, thanks.

Dance when everyone is watching . . . or no one, whatever your vibe is.

Well no shit, genius! What a way to alleviate some of the hardship I'm going through, by being told that it's not really *that* hard. Of course someone has it worse, likely much *much* worse. This just makes me feel sad for them now on top of my own sad, and then feel guilty about my initial sadness, which is snowballing into one big emotional mess. Thanks, champ.

If you've ever been lucky enough to end up in a hospital you will know that this saying is obviously true, but whether it's true or not doesn't exactly make it a comforting thing to hear while you're in a state of suffering. Not often is it helpful in the heat of the moment to learn about some other poor person going through worse shit, so ya gotta wonder why people offer these futile tales of woe during already challenging times. It's a bit strange and possibly the reason some people don't feel safe to speak about their struggles.

You wouldn't fucken run up to somebody who has just stacked their bike, nailed themselves face-first on the concrete and is now crying in pain, only to point to a picture of a war on your phone and exclaim, 'This is worse!' Because that would be super inappropriate, irrelevant, weird and no doubt increase their suffering for multiple reasons. A big one being, of course, that the unwarranted life view from some random gronk who seems to know it all is many flavours of arrogant, don't ya reckon? Being right or having a supposedly interesting story about a similar yet worse time may actually not be a great topic to launch into if you give a shit for a person who is going through some tough moments. Empathy is good shit and doesn't require tales of similarity to practise.

Informing anyone that 'someone has it worse than you' sounds like, 'I don't really give a shit about you and what you're going through, I've seen way more hectic shit go down'. Fucken good for you, legend, we all love that arsehole (commonly a bloke, let's be honest) at the party who's always seen cooler shit than you, done cooler stuff, stacked it harder and been through apparently more than you ever have. They are usually the most irritating person to have around when you're experiencing a tricky time.

I remember spending time in respiratory wards, seeing people across from me desperately out of breath and asking for help to breathe; sometimes they really couldn't be helped with it and I'd think, *fuck, that poor person is suffering a lot*. I have experienced breathlessness like this and know somewhat just how awful and desperate that feeling of drowning in your seat feels. I was just out of major surgery myself, yet for some strange reason I didn't in that moment have the urge to wave down the

MOBILE NEWS

WORSE SHIT

...y in Mobile News more ...rse shit. Reports are ...co... in of worse shit ...ng everywhere, ...in continuing to ...ppen everywhere.

patient in the opposite bed, point to myself and yell, 'Oi bro, at least this shit didn't happen to ya, hey?' Because that would be profoundly insensitive and a shitty thing to do – and what's more, we weren't in comparable situations, because we were each coping with our own uniquely awful hand we'd been dealt. Sure, this other person was in the same ward as me and may well have experienced similar feelings to me at some stage, but our levels of suffering were entirely different and came from two separate lifetimes of distinct experiences.

I also really can't recall any moments of profound suffering in my life where reminding myself of something even worse happening was of any real help.

In my opinion, tattoos are a good example of on-the-ground, non-comparable physical suffering. I've had quite a few over a great deal of my body. I have been getting hammered with them for more than fifteen years now so have plenty of understanding of what the routine is like. If you haven't had a tattoo, DON'T DO IT! 'cause you'll never be able to get a job, rent a car, get a loan or make any new friends ever again because no one will trust you and this new life of crime won't pay. Just kidding, although yes, at times it fucking does hurt, sometimes in more ways than just physical pain. Let me tell ya, once you get tattoos on your neck and hands, some social things change. Mostly I don't give a shit about it and have become used to people crossing the road when I'm walking on the footpath, and have also enjoyed the added adventure of being more interesting to certain officials when travelling through security checkpoints, but by far some of the most painful parts of tattoos are being told relentlessly about the never-gonna-happen tattoos that other people are planning on getting when they are drunk.

But back to the actual tattooing part . . .

When you get a tattoo, you are often in a place where other people are undergoing the same painful experience at the same time, known as a tattoo parlour. A parlour, would you believe? The word parlour seems a somewhat mild one to describe a venue with all the suffering going on inside. It's not uncommon to witness someone else muscling through some quite intense pain in an area of their body that looks very ouchy to have a bunch of needles being fired into their skin approximately ninety times a second. You may even see someone copping a tattoo in the very same place as you but not seeming to give much of a shit about the pain at all. It's quite wild, how much people's pain thresholds vary.

'SOMETIMES SADNESS IS OKAY, IT DOESN'T ALWAYS NEED FIXING, IT JUST NEEDS TO GO FOR A RUN IN THE PADDOCK.'

JULES' TAKE ON PARLOURS

I've always found the word 'parlour' quite sinister,
I think because of the line '"Will you walk into my parlour?"
said the Spider to the Fly' from the poem about a spider
luring a fly with flattery to her death. But that might
just be me, haha.

I have been in this situation a lot first-hand and I think it's
a good example because not only is each person entirely
different from the next – and, sure, will be able to tolerate
different levels of pain – but we're comparing the same
kinda pain that's probably being processed by their mind
and body in distinct ways. I know some people who can
handle a lot of the pain and know what to do with it in their
head; they know to stay calm and breathe and can make it
through quite lengthy amounts of time and tattooing as a
result.

 Then you have someone like me. This may come as a
surprise to you, but I fucken hate being tattooed – I have
even cried during one, and not that long ago. At times the
pain for me is so extreme that I feel physically trapped
and attacked and can get quite emotionally rattled by it.
This isn't the case every time and different spots on my
body are worse than others, but I find anything over an
hour hard to manage. What I find particularly hard is to
stay on top of my mental state during the session. It can be

quite gruelling and traumatic
if I let the pain overwhelm me.
I try to stop it before it gets
to the traumatic part but
sometimes you've come
so far and you're almost
out of the woods
with the design
and don't want to
stress the artist
out, so you bargain
with yourself and
push through. A bit
of calming self-chat can

help but it's a real fucken tough one to listen to.

This is, of course, only my experience. I know a lot of
people who have had their bodies heavily tattooed and while
none of them have loved it heaps, really, their tolerance
suggests to me that what I go through in comparison is
often profound and different to my friends. My guess is that
I have a history of physical pain that's a far cry from some
of theirs, so my relationship to that physical pain and how
it came about is rooted in some pretty heavy, traumatic
times. Maybe this is what makes it seemingly worse for
me than others sometimes? I associate the moment with
bad shit from my past in my head and feel trapped by it.
Yet I still keep doing it! I put myself through it again and

again because I want to look a certain way that makes me happier in the end and ultimately that exchange is worth it. Funny how the younger me had it technically 'worse' back when I started getting tattooed yet that knowledge at the time didn't seem to fucken help. It's not always that bad, but a lot of the time it's a solid whack of pain.

What I'm getting at is that my experience is entirely different to everyone else's at the tattoo parlour – while we do share a common theme of being in pain, for some it's okay and they can cope much better emotionally. What certainly doesn't help is to tell someone in a tattoo chair that getting my throat inked hurt more than their arm will. I reckon we need to let everyone else decide how stressful their experiences are, rather than doing it for them.

So when you see a champion who's in a challenging spot, go ahead and empathise with them and say something *actually* comforting, but remember that comparing an apparently worse time is not likely going to help one bit. Sympathy is nice and all but often the pity party isn't needed as much as a little understanding instead. Trying to put yourself in the other person's shoes for a sec to consider how they might be feeling is the champagne of care. Deciding how someone feels without considering things from their perspective is dangerously at risk of being some pretty useless support, possibly even making it harder for them in the future to talk about what's going on in their lives. There's nothing wrong with having your own perspective on someone's struggles, but to truly give a shit about them it takes a bit of chill-the-fuck-out-and-let-them-tell-ya, rather than dishing out anecdotes about your mate Lori who had that happen to her that one time and how it was so bad, hey. Empathy is like the older, less drunk sibling of sympathy; it has a licence and can even drive to pick you up from the party, whereas sympathy – though it isn't completely devoid of compassion – loves talking about itself for the entire ride home. Being a mate who listens to their mates is a good mate. Dishing out a couple of ripping yarns has its place as good mate stuff, but only when the time is right, and not in place of the listening bit.

Returning to my earlier shit-hanging tirade about this burnt-out saying, who can forget the classic parental way of rounding off 'finish your bloody dinner' with 'there are kids starving in Africa who would love that meal, so finish it'. Great call, associating the kid's relationship with food with guilt, shame and suffering – that won't cause any issues later on, hell no. Don't get me wrong: famine is absolutely heartbreaking and awful and there are lessons to be learnt whenever it happens, but I doubt eating food when you don't want to is a fast track to fighting it and thereby resolving such an enormous problem. Hey, also, I'm not a parent and I don't pretend to know how hard it is to get a little ratbag to eat their food sometimes, so forgive me for chipping in where I don't belong. While I think it's good to acknowledge your privilege and also as a young person to learn about the wider world outside of your home and some of the struggles people on this planet go through, I'm not sure weaponising the remaining uneaten dinner on the plate with a throwaway comment that 'people are starving elsewhere' is the most helpful or accessible way for that info to sink in. It just makes you feel like shit and now ungrateful that you haven't forced another fish finger into your head.

'I RECKON WE NEED TO LET EVERYONE ELSE DECIDE HOW STRESSFUL THEIR EXPERIENCES ARE, RATHER THAN DOING IT FOR THEM.'

It can be confronting seeing someone have a hard go of it and if you don't have anything groundbreaking to say to someone who has been served a dose, that is okay, you're not expected to. Not everything in life is a movie where everyone just says all this well-scripted shit all the time. We don't all have a writers' room scripting everything that is going to happen today and surprise surprise, not all of us are well versed on certain topics because maybe we don't fucken know much about them. Some people are better at comforting people in strife than others, possibly because they've been through a similar thing or are more mentally available to take on that conversation than you are today. That's life for ya: some champions are better at certain shit some days than you are, and that is super fine – not only is it fine, it's fucken great. If we were all off the clock at the same time life would be weird. Sometimes even just having someone try to put themselves in the struggling friend's shoes is all the care that's needed in that moment.

No one's loving it sick, as we all want the moment to be better, but sometimes it just won't get any better. That is a hard place to sit in. Sometimes sadness is okay, it doesn't always need fixing, it just needs to go for a run in the paddock. Feeling like shit is one of those things that is fucking annoying but kinda has to happen so we don't feel as shit later on – hopefully the shitness levels are manageable, but for some they will be a lot.

I know I've had some putrid moments in my life where I thought I couldn't possibly feel any worse, truly any worse. I felt like the entire world was trying to fucken stick it to me from every direction, with no way to escape. I remember in some of these moments a person who cared for me would sit with me, put a hand on my back and say something along the lines of, 'Yeah this is pretty shit', and it would feel just a little easier. It was nice to have them there even though I was all weird in my body and had no response to the comforting gesture except more tears as I got through it at my own pace. What mattered most at that time was having someone accept me as I was, and while I didn't need validating, I appreciated the lack of bogus comparisons to anyone else's suffering. I think you often remember the feeling more of having people physically present when you go through tough times and less of the exact things they say to you. Being a support to a champion suffering a tough time isn't always poetic and smooth and sometimes you say the same shit over and over again, or it means going around in conversational circles back to the spot where you started, but there is care in there – it matters and it's there.

JULES' TAKE ON SOMEONE HAVING IT WORSE

Nat is the best person ever. Truly, so caring, so honest, so talented, so loving. If you're reading this you might love him too, and I'm sure you also have friends who struggle in a similar way, or a partner, or you do yourself. By contrast, I'm a pretty happy-go-lucky person. I have my moments, of course, but I am fortunate enough not to have to battle my head too badly just to exist.

It's really hard when the person you care about most in the world is clearly in distress – all you want to do is rid the universe of whatever it is that is causing them pain and make it stop. Immediately.

But there are no 'fixes' here. Mental health is a fickle
and unpredictable beast. It won't be reasoned with, and
sometimes it won't even be contained. As much as your
impulse might be to try to logic your loved one's way out,
it's often not going to be possible. Feeling powerless but
so desperate to help can be kinda devastating.

One thing I've learnt is that listening, truly listening, is a
superpower. Sometimes solutions aren't what people need.
Be present, and if something is tough, be onside. Not to
your own detriment, of course, but if your loved one tells
you something is sucky, then yeah – it sucks.

Sometimes just being there and caring is the only thing
you can do. Often, it's also the best thing.

Hey, maybe you or your mate want to be alone with the
struggle for a while. I reckon that shit is alright, too. I have
spent many nights cranking The Dirty Three with just my
own company and letting the tears flow like a fucken Super
Soaker – a good cry is quite cathartic, especially with a sad
song to give it a little extra kick in the arse. Spending a bit
of solo time to feel out your struggles is pretty valuable and
has the bonus that no other surprise sympathy is allowed
in to tell you what you feel. I've always found that kinda
funny after a good solo meltdown – realising that I was a
little bit of a mess and God, what a scene I'd made – but I
suppose it doesn't matter 'cause the only person to witness
it was myself. I've kind of accidentally programmed myself

to crack the sad and have possibly ruined The Dirty Three's music for myself now, as I have to make an effort not to spontaneously cry when it comes on, lol.

All of which is to say: I don't believe that someone else's struggles invalidate anything you might be going through, and I certainly don't reckon ya have to be a well-spoken hero to comfort someone suffering in their jocks.

Maybe just sometimes we can afford to piss off the whole 'someone else has it worse' headspace and set the goalposts somewhere closer to self-care and understanding for not just yourself but for how it must feel for that mate of yours having a Barry. And while we're there, maybe even how you helped them feel a little better by being a champion who was listening and being a fucken legend for giving an empathetic shit. Chats about tough stuff are so very right-on, as is being there to support the person who's in need of one.

Someone has it *different* to you and that's what matters more than it being worse. Truly none of our experiences are gonna be exactly the same, hence why listening is so fucken awesome and helpful. We are but snowflakes in this complicated, tricky life and that's what makes this all so interesting, occasionally confusing and sad, and sometimes fucken good fun.

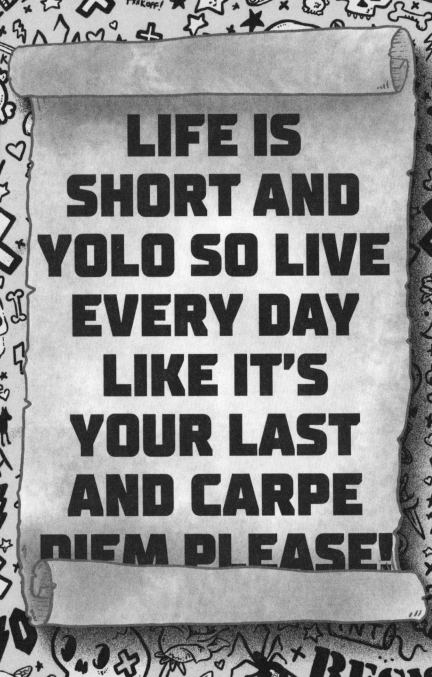

Fuck, I've heard 'Life is short' so many times in my medium-length life and it's bothered me every single time.

No, it's not.

The saying 'life is short' bothers me because it's so relative; some things only live for a few hours of a single day, so in comparison unless you're talking to a mayfly then you're possibly a little off. Without going full self-appointed-life-coach energy on you here, I think this is the most glass-half-empty shit of a cliché out there. I know it's a bold call, but someone had to do it. Sure, life is short if you die young, which is awfully sad and horrible for obvious reasons, but otherwise, let's be honest, it goes for a fucking long time – like years and years and years, literally.

Have you ever had to sit through an instructional video on how to put together a piece of furniture, or attended an eight-hour safety course for work to learn shit you already know? Remember listening to that mind-numbingly self-indulgent arsehole giving an award acceptance speech that made you feel as if it was never going to end? This alone is proof to me that life goes for ages.

I realise that intentionally frustrating yourself with boring shit isn't a great way to live your life, but time is one of those things that just fucken happens, like compost and getting older. You can buy a convertible, pierce your ear and pretend it's not happening but, sorry champ, it just is, there's nothing you can do about it – and it's taking its literal time doing it.

Now, as someone with a super anxious mind who is frustrated constantly that I haven't done enough today or done 'the thing' right, I agree that there are occasionally moments when time really is of the essence, when a little bit of hustle can't hurt. I know this from trying to write, film and edit a video for my channel all before a Friday afternoon drop: gotta move it to get that time slot! I also know what it is to feel comfortable in doing just about nothing, and not always for a great reason. I have surprisingly quite sharp and difficult memories of being a chronic weed smoker as a teenager and all the way into my early twenties, and have reflected on how much time I wasted sitting on my arse doing fuck-all, just being . . . stoned. There can be serious amounts of CBF energy going on when you're in that space – chuck in some outstanding fears of the universe, mental health problems and an actual physical illness, and I managed to do a fair amount of very little for quite a long time . . . like months on end. It felt like years. Much to the frustration of friends and family, I would spend a great deal of my life back then hiding from society, really just trying to cope with the world around me the best way I could for that day/week/month.

Isn't it funny that when you're a kid, all you want is to be old enough to do the cool shit the older ones get to do? Ya can't wait to turn ten, the big 'double digits'; then ya can't wait to be a teenager from there, onwards and upwards till you're sixteen to get your learner licence, and then eighteen when you can go to pubs and clubs. Then shit changes and you suddenly start to want the reverse, for some reason. What the fuck happened? I remember beginning to become scared of the next year coming as I got older in my twenties, counting the months backwards from my birthday to how old I was today, thinking, *Well I'm twenty-two for another four months, so I can relax; I'll do the grown-up stuff when I'm twenty-three.* I remember being so fucken worried about not being a teenager anymore and thinking that turning twenty made me 'old'. To be honest, a great deal of me didn't think I was gonna live past twenty until I got there. I almost didn't, to be fair, but not for the reasons I thought – a bit of TB was working its magic on that end.

Every fucking year I got older in my twenties I had some stupid number in my head that represented a deadline for getting my shit together. None of those deadlines were ever met – like *none* of them. I'd heard about the so-called twenty-seven club where all the rock stars die aged twenty-seven, and was sure it was gonna be my new deadline. Giving myself a bit of rockstar status there, eh? Well, that didn't happen either, and so now what? Life goes on, I suppose. By the time my thirtieth came around I was so exhausted by freaking out about my age that I didn't even bother celebrating it. It felt like the final frontier, which is kinda ridiculous and hilarious all at once.

'I'VE BEEN TO A FEW PARTIES WHERE I'VE FELT LIKE I'M GOING AT YOLO SPEED AND FEEL LUCKY TO HAVE MADE IT TO THE NEXT DAY.'

Something ticked over in my brain at that stage and I realised that I didn't give a fuck what age I was. Don't ask me why. I think maybe I'd just worked out that there's no stopping it, and thinking about how much gnarly shit had happened in my life by that point made me glad it was behind me. No desire to go back and have another crack at it, thanks. Youth may be wasted on the young, but that's fine, they can have it: fuck going through that all again!

I remember being a bit taken aback once when my mate – who has only a few years on me – told me he was pumped to get older. I asked why he thought so, and he replied, 'Because you just don't give a fuck when you're old'. Makes total sense: the further I get through life, the less I give a shit about a lot of petty issues. Doesn't mean I'm not still riddled with panic and anxiety daily, but it's different stuff now, less about what Keiran and Stacy got busted doing up the back of the bus and more about bigger-picture shit like how I'm going to look after myself better and boring shit like paying rent. I dunno if it's better to let go of my fascination with the passage of time, but it's less messy in many ways.

The concept of 'living every day like it's your last' is one that makes none of that previous shit any better. In fact, being told 'This could be your last day on this planet and you could get hit by a bus tomorrow' is such an extra way of encouraging people to think about how our time here is finite. Sure, you *could* get hit by a bus tomorrow, but the chances are you won't, so don't feel like you can't cross any roads tomorrow, okay?

It gets idealised, the 'last day on Earth', as if you're gonna just fucken go for it and suddenly live your best life in twenty-four hours. Get fucked, no you fucken won't! You'll probably sit there shitting yourself with fear about your imminent demise, crying rather than going skydiving nude or whatever is on your bucket list. I've been to a few parties where I've felt like I'm going at YOLO speed and feel lucky to have made it to the next day. And I tell ya what, it's not the joyous life-affirming memory that it's supposed to be.

YOLO – to explain to the three people on Earth who may not know what this overused acronym means: 'You only live once' – well, it has quite the reputation for going badly. There's a story about a twenty-one-year-old fella in the States who in the early 2000s famously was drink-driving at high speed while tweeting 'Driving tweeting sipping the cup #fuckit yolo I'm turning it up' and proceeded to fly through a red light and slam his car into a wall, killing himself and all his mates in the car. Very fucking sad. There's a lot wrong with that situation, one of them being this whole YOLO thing. Yes, you do only live once but you can go a bit too hard and end up fucking yourself up in the process. I am hardly someone who hasn't gone too hard at all, in fact several times in my life I have almost taken myself out. I rode a fucken 1000cc motorcycle for a long time, for fuck's sake. Anyone who rides a motorbike knows what I mean. I have lost a best mate in a flash on one too, a heartbreaking moment I won't ever forget.

The idea that you can slow down and take a breath is one that has been hugely valuable for me to try to take on board. There's only so much Carpe sliding into your own Diems that you can really do in any given diem, and hey – your diem might be a hard one to carpe given all that's in front of you.

'YOUTH MAY BE WASTED ON THE YOUNG, BUT THAT'S FINE, THEY CAN HAVE IT: FUCK GOING THROUGH THAT ALL AGAIN!'

A bit of yahoo shit is good fun, but there is a line in the sand where you can come on too strong and blow a valve trying to live your best life. There's a lot to be said about fun via measured risk and what that means to each person. Part of growing up is ya gotta sometimes learn the hard way what taking risk means and how to be a little smarter about it. Being adventurous is not a bad thing when done with a little style and finesse. Being force-fed heaps of extreme sports on the TV while you've been having a shit go sitting at work all week can really set the bar unnecessarily high.

Doing stupid, risky shit is kinda fun but it can be a dangerously addictive escapist level of fun when trying to fill a gap elsewhere in your life. Doing a backflip off a cliff to forget your ex sounds like a great distraction and all, but it's not gonna make the memory of her go away, Kenneth. There are levels of excitement that I personally don't want to know about, and that's one of them. I don't need to sit on a gold-plated toilet with fireworks going off in it after just free diving the Mariana Trench to finally

say I experienced today to the fullest.

I have so many metaphors for over-living life. Imagine life is a kebab, for example. Have you ever been so hungry that you ordered a kebab with everything on it? Like, I mean fucken everything – all the sauces, all the meats, all the cheese and all the salads. Dammit, you even got hot chips bashed into it. I guarantee there was so much on it that it was intolerable and barely edible.

I get that some people just wanna go flat stick through life and experience all it has to offer, and though I think that's humanly impossible, it's good to have some of that positive mental attitude and go get 'em if your head allows that level of intensity. But telling someone else that they need to 'live today like it's their last' might actually be a massive kick in the guts if their last day is spent having to go to work in retail with rude customers doing their head in or having to hang out at a photocopier while a douchebag barks orders at them. (Sorry, Donna.)

'MAYBE SWAP THE YOLO FOR YO, CHILL!'

ALTERNATIVE ACTIVITIES TO HAVING TO CARPE DIEM OR YOLO

Carpe Chillax

Fucken seize a bit of a chill pill turbo.

RAMBO

Relaxing Afternoons May Be Organised.

YOGO

It couldn't be more chilled if it tried. It's literally just a brand of yoghurt and asks a lot less of you.

RDO

Rostered Day Off may not be my acronym, but still, try that.

BOGOF

Buy One Get One Free!

LIAISE

Life Is Already Intensely Stressful Enough.

Relaxat Est In Horto

All the Latin students out there will know immediately that you're letting them know 'You'll be chillin' in the garden.'

There's already so much overstimulating guilt being slingshotted at you every day via your phone, telling you you're not doing enough with your life, without some blowhard telling you to live more. Maybe swap the YOLO for Yo, chill! A little calming of the farm might actually be a much more healthy and accessible option than highway-surfing the roof of a Commodore.

Like listening to someone who has just done a round-the-world trip and won't shut the fuck up about how much 'YOU HAVE TO GO, SARAH, *OMG*!', I reckon you can say a polite no to living life as if it was on meth.

Why the massive hurry? Last week you didn't even BASE-jump off a bridge in France and you were okay. Sure, your heart rate wasn't as concerningly high as a result, but you can always just watch *Ozark* and achieve a panic attack that's equally intense without having to leave your seat.

If YOLO is indeed true, then what are you supposed to achieve in the 'LO' part of YOLO? Are you supposed to have done all the things by then? Have you worked out the meaning of life during this time and will you die a fucken glowing star of 'Told you this was the right way!'?

Or will it look more like: 'Yeah, that was pretty good' and everything ended up good enough? The aspirations of adventure and desires versus what will actually happen in your life won't always match up, but that surely is a common enough story that it's okay not to get all the things you ever wanted like some lotto ad? A moderate level of adventure can be a good life gap-filler, but what those adventures turn out to be are entirely up to you.

If you knew you had a limited amount of time left, would that change what you had planned? Or would you still go to the pub later, eat a parmy, come home late, spend tomorrow hungover and watching rubbish television? Your call (and a good parmy is pretty great, just saying). Maybe going out with some glorious bang is actually adding unnecessary pressure and making this whole YOLO thing super stressful.

I reckon youse should do what youse feel like doing, when you feel up for doing it. Fuck what the bus stop ad says, with all those pretend smiling faces on it – do you at your speed. Live every day how you want.

Like I was saying earlier, this life shit goes for ages unless you Carpe too much Diem at once. Ease up turbo, you got this.

FINAL SHIT SAYINGS SHOWDOWN

There are actually thousands of dogshit sayings that make no sense to me, but if I wrote a chapter on each of them this book would be as long as the Bible. So here are a handful of spareys I had lying around that I wanted to squeeze in for a power round:

TIME HEALS ALL

No it doesn't. It's actually just time.

PUT UP AND SHUT UP

How about 'Nah, fuck this shit, I'm out'?

DON'T KNOCK IT TILL YA TRY IT

There are a million things I'm happy to knock without trying. Drinking brake fluid, for one.

ALWAYS GRAB A DISCOUNT

Don't get me wrong, I love a good discount, but retreaded tyres are not actually that safe. Sometimes, spend the money.

QUIT WORRYING

Try compassion instead, ya brick wall.

CHANGE IS AS GOOD AS A HOLIDAY

Not if that holiday is shit.

SHOOT FOR THE MOON. EVEN IF YOU MISS, YOU'LL LAND AMONG THE STARS

Stars are a lot fucken further away than the moon and you will immediately burn to death if you come even close to one.

THE GRASS IS GREENER ON THE OTHER SIDE

That's actually called astroturf and it's not real.

WORK HARD, PLAY HARD

Work Less, PlayStation.

HE WHO FEARS DEATH WILL NEVER DO ANYTHING WORTHY OF A MAN WHO IS ALIVE

Well then, if that isn't the biggest load of shit I've ever read I don't know what is. Do I need to explain why this is shit?

NO USE CRYING OVER SPILT MILK

That was the last of the milk and I have had a really tough time getting myself out of bed to make that coffee. Tears are happening and you can't stop me.

LOOK ON THE BRIGHT SIDE

Of this shattered collarbone that I got in the first week of my holiday in Thailand? This has actually fucked the whole trip. Where's the shiny bit I'm supposed to be looking at, sorry?

IF YOU CAN'T BEAT 'EM, JOIN 'EM

What a shit idea. Every football team would be chat except for just one if that were true.

IF YOU DON'T HAVE ANYTHING NICE TO SAY THEN SAY NOTHING AT ALL

My career would literally be immediately over if I did that.

GREAT THINGS NEVER COME FROM COMFORT ZONES

Um, yes they do. It's called a bubble bath and it's awesome, so you can leave.

CHECK YA LATER, SKATER

So there it is champion, a whole bunch of what 'Nat' – or not – to do. I can't help but feel like I've given a shitload of suggestions on what not to do, so maybe just to close it out I'll break the rules and suggest three things that you *could* do when faced with the challenges of life's tough times.

1. Be kind to yourself, and don't be too fucken hard on yourself. Forgive yourself for not doing everything perfectly – we fuck up, it's human nature (not the band). Working on doing better is important, as is listening, and this includes to yourself, champion.

2. Talk about how you feel, all the time, like heaps and heaps, because you're a fucken champion who deserves to talk stuff out with people who care about you. And later on, when you feel up for it, ask ya mates how they're going too. Check in with the people you love 'cause it can really help, even when they are doing okay. Never has that shit failed me, and the more I do it the less trapped in my busy head nonsense I feel.

3. The next time some entitled shithead tells you to smile, you could reply with your middle finger and a 'No thanks, fuckwit, I'll be right' and then just feel out your feelings as you were on your own terms in a much healthier way.

Look, I'm not trying to be some fucken life coach here. The absolute truth of the matter is that a lot of the time I'm a just a high-functioning mess. I've even needed to take several meltdown breaks from writing this book. I'm certainly no mental health expert, but I do encourage people to talk to one from time to time. I'm still very much learning what I need to do to get through this very bloody strange and complex universe; talking about it and taking the piss out of a few things along the way has really helped.

It's never going to sit well with me being told that I need to have good vibes or smile more. I think more of this regurgitated false positivity stuff needs to get in the bin or get a bit more genuine, and it should certainly stop shouting at us all so much.

Not every bit of advice is good advice, not all help is helpful. And not all beach houses need to have wooden signs inside them that say 'Beach' for me to know it's down the street, either.

Thank you so much for reading my book. I am truly grateful for your time and support. I think you're great and that you should smile just as much as you fucken want to 'cause you're in charge of what you do with your own face.

Don't take shit from stupid fucken cringe signage or dickheads who don't know what the fuck they're talking about.

Love ya guts. Till next time, keep those vibes complex!

CONTRIBUTORS

Julia Gee

Jules is Nat's creative accomplice and cackle chorus on Nat's What I Reckon, as well as his off-screen partner in crime. A designer by trade, Jules is responsible for the channel's graphics and most merchandise designs, and has added cinematographer extraordinaire and book co-conspirator to her assorted string of creative titles. When she's not getting artsy, she can often be found indulging her love of cheese and *RuPaul's Drag Race* (the two are inseparable), cuddling her house chickens (ragdoll cats), dancing (badly) or playing drums. Follow her behind-the-scenes adventures at 📷 @holy_bat_syllables and her art at 📷 @housechickenstudios.

Bunkwaa

Bunkwaa is an Australian comic book artist, animator and illustrator. His art is a sleight-of-hand journey into hyper-cartoon worlds, a kaleidoscopic ride full of character, worlds within worlds and faces within faces. You can connect with him at 📷 @bunkwaa and learn more about his latest projects at bunkwaa.com.

RESOURCES

Lifeline
13 11 14
lifeline.org.au

Beyond Blue
1300 22 4636
beyondblue.org.au

headspace
1800 650 890
headspace.org.au

ReachOut
au.reachout.com

Suicide Call Back Service
1300 659 467
suicidecallbackservice.org.au

Griefline
1300 845 745
griefline.org.au

Australian Centre for Grief and Bereavement
grief.org.au

ACKNOWLEDGEMENTS

Firstly, thanks to Jules, my main gal, for chucking in a few awesome comments in the book and helping me work out what the fuck I'm trying to say half the time. But mostly for sticking with me and caring for me when my head is being a nasty fuckwit.

Huge bloody thanks to Izzy and Clive as always for believing in me and the bananas shit I come up with: thanks for helping me to keep creating cool books, you're true bloody champions. Adam, mate, thanks for your sick graphic design and Jedi-level layout skills.

Big yeeeeeew to my management and agent super crew Tom, Andrew and Julie. Thanks for holding my entertainment hand through all these crazy years.

Oi Bunkwaa, my dude – you have fucking nailed the art in this book and once again fucking smashed it. Love ya.

To you the reader, the champion, the amazing person you are, thanks for supporting me and laughing at my jokes. Thanks for voting for my books in awards and telling ya mates about what I do.

Finally, I want to express my very serious gratitude to all the people in my life who have been patient and supportive of me and my difficult mental health struggles while I try to work out what the fuck is going on. I really appreciate the chats, the love, the tears, the hugs and the online lockdown hangs.

Thanks for having my back.

Bloody champions, the lot of ya.

SEE YOU ON THE INTERNET, CHAMPION